WHAT PEOPLE ARE SAYING ABOUT ALEX PEYKOFF AND *THE SATISFACTION GUARANTEE*

Brilliant, insightful, and straight to the point. Alex Peykoff has given us magic keys that can change lives quickly! If you struggle to ditch the lame excuses that keep you from achieving your dreams, then *The Satisfaction Guarantee* is a must! I love this book!

—Ron Browning
Voice Coach to the Stars

My dear friend and mentor, Alex, has the greatest heart, and his power to connect and network has been a game changer for me. He's helped me get on more stages. He's helped me launch my jewelry line. He's helped me write my book. So, if you're looking for a coach to help you get to the next level, Alex is your person. Let him guide you, lead you, and connect you to get your life to the next level.

—Yvonne Dellos
FNP, MSN, Serial Entrepreneur

Over the years, I've learned that it's vital to surround yourself with the right people and the right ideas. And that's why I surround myself with people like Alex Peykoff. He wrote *The Satisfaction Guarantee*, which will give you some insight into what it's like to be his friend. He's an amazing individual who will help change the way you look at things, and as Wayne Dyer says, "If you change the way you look at things, the things you look at change." Check out this book, hang out, follow him, and most of all, ask him for help, because he loves to be of service and of value.

—David Meltzer
Speaker, Author, Entrepreneur

I support Alex Peykoff and his entire crew because what they're doing is very needed, but most importantly, it helps elevate everybody's life so they can have a Satisfied Life.

—Sharon Lechter, C.P.A.
Entrepreneur, International Speaker, Bestselling Author

My trusted friend and advisor Alex Peykoff simply defines the word empath on every level. You should try living a fulfilling life that you cannot buy. Living in the now is what Alex teaches, and that is one of the key principles of an abundant existence on all levels.

—Tex Caldarola
CEO of White Knight Global Partners

I heard Alex speak at an event at Sofi Stadium in California. He spoke with so much purposeful passion that it made the hair stand up on my arms.

—Darren Prince
CEO of Prince Marketing Group

I love Alex's message and could talk for hours about these topics. Thank you for your positive words; they go a long way, especially during tough times.

—**Elizabeth Massing**
Chief Human Resources Officer at 14 West
& the Agora Companies

I can't thank Alex enough for seeing me, for believing in what we do, and for trying to help. It means the world to me. I'm beyond grateful to him for being authentic and vulnerable.

—**Christina Simos**
Executive Director of Friendly House

Alex Peykoff was the catalyst that opened up my universe. This is the true essence of what his book offers. His book stands out above the rest as he's able to dive right into what we all struggle with and get to the heart of the solutions so that we can live a Satisfied Life!

—**Danica Vorkapich Patton**
Pasadena, CA

THE
SATISFACTION
GUARANTEE

*Redefine Wealth, Become Emotionally
Debt-Free, and Unlock True Fulfillment*

ALEX PEYKOFF

WITH KATHY HASKINS

THE SATISFACTION GUARANTEE

Redefine Wealth, Become Emotionally Debt-Free, and Unlock True Fulfillment

For permission requests, speaking inquiries, and bulk order purchase options, email: alex@mysatisfiedlife.com

SATISFIED LIFE
668 N Coast Hwy #305
Laguna Beach, CA 92651

Scribe: Kathy Haskins| KathyHaskins.com
Editor: Lori Lynn Enterprises | LoriLynnEnterprises.com
Design: Transcendent Publishing | TranscendentPublishing.com

ISBN: 979-8-9911569-8-1

True satisfaction comes from within, when you have peace in your heart and contentment in your soul.

—ANONYMOUS

Do not look for luxury in watches or bracelets, do not look for luxury in forks or sails.

Luxury is laughter and friends. luxury is rain on your face, luxury is hugs and kisses.

Don't look for luxury in shops, don't look for it in gifts, don't look for it at parties, don't look for it at events.

Luxury is being loved by people, luxury is being respected, luxury is having parents, luxury is being able to play with your grandchildren, luxury is what money can't buy.

—CLINT EASTWOOD

CONTENTS

For Mia,
With all my love.

In loving memory of Don,
(3/18/1948 – 8/14/2024)
You have forever changed my life.

In loving memory of my mom, Jean Kellner Thoms
(8/11/40 - 10/11/24)
Thank you for your constant love. You taught me how
to love Mia unconditionally, and all I ever needed was
the love you gave.

FOREWORD

I met Alex and his daughter Mia in 2014 when a mutual friend introduced us at one of my events. We connected immediately. He was a single father raising Mia by himself, and I could see he had his priorities right. We talked about our families, our work, and what kind of impact we wanted to make. Alex was so genuine and easy to talk to, and it became apparent in a very short time that we had the same values. It wasn't long before we became real friends, not just acquaintances.

Alex spent time with me at more of my events, and it has always impressed me how, despite coming from a legendary family in the business world, he can still put all pretense aside and treat everyone he meets with genuine respect. Alex has a huge heart. He goes all-in, unconditionally, in everything he does. Alex shows people that he cares and makes them feel safe enough to open up and have a deep conversation about the things that are truly in their hearts. He has a gift of connecting with people—of being a bridge builder.

Alex's perspective is unique in the personal development world. He comes from a world of success, money, and achievement, and has first-hand experience that money doesn't solve all problems. Money simply doesn't equal happiness, peace, and satisfaction.

People don't *want* to hear that, but they *need* to hear it. Money may not bring satisfaction, but healing our emotional debt brings that and more. In this book, you'll find that he is redefining the meaning of wealth.

At my events, I can hand him the mic and trust him to greet everyone and share a message. I believe that God didn't create any of us to be average. We're called to be extraordinary and step into the full power that God's given us. Alex's message is a beautiful complement to mine, and he shares fundamental tools to live out our true callings in this life. Through his personal stories and powerful life lessons, he teaches us how to live the life we long for.

Alex inspires people to lay aside society's demands and expectations and get in touch with who they really want to be. He encourages them to feel, to experience, and to truly live. His ability to bring out the best in people is amazing. He's teaching people how to live a Satisfied Life and making a huge impact in this world. Many world shakers and history makers, people living uncommon lives, live the life Alex teaches.

You have to have uncommon plans and uncommon desires but also uncommon discipline. Learn from an uncommon man.

Alex Peykoff will teach you how to live a Satisfied Life. He's a great mentor and friend, and it's a privilege to be on this journey of life with him.

—Tim Storey
Author, Speaker, and "The Original Comeback Coach"

INTRODUCTION

> "True satisfaction is not measured by the wealth
> you accumulate, but by the impact you make
> on the lives of others."
>
> — ANONYMOUS

"**N**o matter how much success I have, I keep coming up empty."

Those words played over and over in Sarah's mind as she checked on the passengers in the first-class cabin, which was full but quiet that night. Most were spending their time unwinding from the day by reading, watching a movie, or scrolling through social media.

Over the gentle hum of the engines taking them home, two men sat side by side, engrossed in conversation. Sarah, being the only one up and moving about, couldn't help but overhear them.

She learned that the two were on their way home from a master-mind event, and both ran thriving businesses. Later, she discovered that the younger man was grieving. His father had recently passed away.

As he spoke of his dad, he mentioned that people had begun to approach him and share their stories about how his father had made them feel safe and valued. Then, he turned to the man beside him, who appeared to be about twenty years his senior, and said, "You remind me so much of my dad." His voice quivered with emotion as tears welled up in his eyes.

For a while, the older man just listened. He seemed to understand that this passenger needed someone to really hear him.

As Sarah came by with another round of margaritas, she watched as these two men connected deeply instead of ignoring each other or making small talk. She overheard bits of the conversation as they continued to share stories about their businesses and families.

Once they landed and were about to exit the plane, she asked the younger man about his flight. What he said surprised her.

"That man saved my life."

What was so special about that conversation that it would end up saving a man's life?

I was able to find out because I was the older man in the story and the host of the mastermind event that Mike had attended. Weeks later, as I was boarding another flight with the same crew, the flight attendant asked me about my friend and told me what he said to her.

I had learned from that brief conversation that even though he had had a good relationship with his dad, Mike felt like he had been a disappointment. He described his battle with drug and alcohol abuse because he didn't know how to deal with that feeling of letting his dad down. It was too late to change anything.

He talked about his wife and newborn baby. His wife was upset with him because they were in the middle of a move when he decided to hop on a plane and attend my mastermind with other successful entrepreneurs. "I'm trying so hard," he said, "but I'm afraid of losing everything because I can't see what's broken, and I can't fix what I can't see."

I had a rare vantage point, both being old enough to be his dad, and growing up with a dad who was financially successful but emotionally unavailable. I grew up believing that the way to safety was through prosperity.

Growing up around people the world deems successful opened my eyes to a reality few people truly understand. You can be worth millions but also be emotionally bankrupt. Money is an excellent tool but a terrible master. And I was watching this young man go down the same path I had seen so many others take before him.

During our conversation, I shared that I had been through many struggles myself, and drawing from my past life lessons, I could offer a different viewpoint. As Mike began to look through the eyes of both his father and his wife, his perspective shifted. He went from feeling empty to having hope in the span of a few hours.

I meet people like Mike all the time. Men and women who are "successful" but unhappy. They're broken in their relationships and in their lives in general. They have lost touch with their emotions and their ability to form genuine connections because they have bought into the lie that accumulating wealth and achieving success would solve all their problems.

Our society glamorizes and celebrates success, bombarding us with messages about what it means to be successful, usually focused entirely on material possessions and achievements. It's always about the car you drive, the designer watch (or shoes, or purse, or whatever) you have, the house you live in, the title you hold, or the degree you earn.

Growing up, I was no stranger to these cultural expectations. My parents, like many others, had their own definitions of success, and they made sure I understood and measured up to their standards. But here's the truth I've learned along the way: success, as defined by others, isn't what really matters at all.

I've had the privilege of getting to know countless successful business owners and entrepreneurs who, by society's standards, are "crushing it." My first-hand experience with these notable people has taught me one thing: chasing someone else's idea of success will leave you feeling empty.

I no longer chase success—or what the world defines as success. Instead, I've started chasing satisfaction. And that has led to a deeply fulfilling life.

How do you chase satisfaction? That's what this book is about. *The Satisfaction Guarantee* is a roadmap to the Satisfied Life, which is a life worth living.

Who Is Alex Peykoff

I am the son of Jean Kellner and Andrew Peykoff Sr., the founder of the world's largest private bottling company. From a young age, as the third brother among eight boys in a blended family, I had to walk a very straight and tight line.

Love and validation were conditional and doled out based on personal achievement. I learned how to work hard and solve problems, and how to get the job done. How to never quit. How to sort through all the bullshit and make good business decisions.

In other words, my dad taught me how to be "successful."

But showing vulnerability was frowned upon, and tears were seen as a display of weakness. In our world, there was simply no room for emotional vulnerability.

Growing up like this, I felt that the goalposts for approval were constantly being moved. I became a shell of myself, performing according to someone else's agenda and doing what they wanted me to do in order to get their validation and love.

As an adult, I decided to live differently. I yearned to discover my true self, to uncover the depths of my emotions while still embracing strength and resilience. I wanted to be fully aware and present in my life.

This decision came in 1999 when a beautiful little miracle named Mia entered my life. My daughter, who was unplanned, turned out to be the light of my life, the greatest gift, and the reason why my whole world would forever be changed. My daughter transformed me, and she is the reason why I am who I am today.

Becoming a "Dadom"

I was 36 years old and living a life that many would envy when I met a captivating woman, and we started dating. But as fate would have it, our relationship was as complicated as we were. Deep down, I knew it was never going to survive.

But a positive pregnancy test changed everything. We had created the spark of a new life, an innocent being. Neither of us felt ready to bring a child into this world. The relationship felt doomed, and as much as I hate to admit it now, I didn't even want to be a father. To be honest, I had no interest in it whatsoever.

Until I heard my baby's heartbeat.

It was a divine moment that made my whole body tingle from head to toe. I thought, *Oh my God, there's a human being growing in there!* God blessed me with this child, and I was going to do everything to make sure she was okay. It was time to make some serious changes.

At 11:02 p.m. on December 7, 1999, this gorgeous little girl made her entrance, and my whole world stopped. Wow! Whatever I had heard, whatever I had learned in my life, none of it mattered. I only wanted to make sure she was unconditionally loved and could be the best version of herself.

I wanted to be better. A better businessman, a better person, but most importantly, I wanted to be the best frickin' father in the world to this baby girl. She gave me that permission slip to change, to break free from old patterns and embrace a new way of living.

As my relationship with Mia's mother came to an end, I found myself in a long and painful custody battle (I'll share more about that later). Thankfully, my mom stepped in to help me raise Mia. My mother had always been in touch with her feminine, emotional side, but she never could express it in our family.

Even as a child, her mother had told her never to let a man see her cry—it was a sign of weakness—so her feelings had always been stifled, and her marriage to my dad eventually failed. Despite her heartbreak, she poured her energy into helping me raise her grand-daughter. During this time, my mom began to truly shine.

With her guidance, I began to tap into my emotions and embrace vulnerability. I had to assume the roles of both mother and father in order to be there for my daughter's every need. I became a "Dadom," learning how to navigate the realm of emotions alongside my little girl.

I don't think I would've known how amazing unconditional love is until I helped to create a life. My emotions started to come alive. I started living life with intentionality and presence, fully feeling all the emotions that came my way. Whatever I did, I was going to do it 100%, and I was going to lead by example. I was all in.

I started to become an expert at being me.

Before Mia entered my life, I often shut down my emotions out of fear. I would avoid pain and hurt, thinking it would protect me.

But let me tell you, as someone who has transformed from a life of emotional detachment to embracing the full spectrum of human experience, there is far more pain in not feeling and far more regret in only half-living.

The paradox lies in the fact that the more in touch we are with our emotions, the stronger we become.

Who This Book Is For

It takes immense courage to face our vulnerabilities head-on. But it is the only way to discover our true power, resilience, and authenticity.

I've encountered countless individuals who may be successful on the financial front but are broken emotionally. Their relationships are shattered, and deep down, they're living a life that doesn't align with their true desires.

People aren't doing things that they really want to do. They're doing what culture or their friends are telling them to do. They fear diving into their own authentic existence because it means confronting their emotions head-on. It means engaging in raw, truthful, and honest conversations with themselves and others.

And unfortunately, even the *thought* of that is terrifying for the average person. So they live their lives conforming to society's expectations and accolades, forgetting their agenda and their truth, and they end up compromising their integrity every step of the way.

This way of life doesn't feel right, but they don't want to deal with the real problem. Instead, they bury their true selves beneath the shiny facades of Lamborghinis, big homes, money, or vices like adultery, porn, or drugs and alcohol.

I've experienced both sides of the spectrum, and I can tell you that hiding behind vices and status symbols is no way to truly live.

People who form their identity around what they do or what they own are missing the best parts of life. They measure their worth solely based on external achievements, and, in doing so, they overlook the richness and depth of life's true treasures. Money is merely a tool, not our identity. Success is nice, but it's never guaranteed. It's dangerous to wrap your happiness around the illusion of success.

But let me ask you this: Can you engage in something and genuinely feel satisfied without being fixated on society's expectations? Can you navigate this journey we call life without compromising your integrity? Can you develop beautiful, deep, and fulfilling relationships that nourish your heart, soul, and mind?

The rules and achievement levels society sets for success ... they're all bullshit. Our upside-down society will try to dictate what success looks like, and that picture keeps changing like the wind.

But society can't dictate what satisfaction should look like, and that's precisely why I talk so much about its importance. Satisfaction is a personal journey. You—and only you—get to determine the definition.

Together, let's unlock the doors to a world where genuine fulfillment awaits you. It's time to go 100% all-in on your life, being fully human, and knowing that it's more than okay to be flawed. It's okay to be unapologetically YOU in every sense of the word.

The life you were meant to live—a life of depth, connection, and unshakable satisfaction—is on the other side of developing your emotional intelligence, practicing gratitude in every situation (even the tough ones), and experiencing authentic connections in your relationships.

As we journey toward unshakeable satisfaction, let's begin by reawakening, experiencing, and embracing the full spectrum of emotions.

CHAPTER 1

ESCAPING A MONOCHROME EXISTENCE

"Abundance is not something we acquire.
It is something we tune into."

—WAYNE DYER

For the longest time, I went through life like a zombie from *Dawn of the Dead*.

Although I've always been an emotional guy, I was told over and over as a young man that any expression of emotion was a sign of weakness. Eventually, I completely shut my feelings down and mindlessly did whatever work was put in front of me.

I wasn't living in the moment. I wasn't present. What was there to be present for? I just had to do the task, not *experience* it. My job was a destination, not an adventure, and life was a monotonous cycle, not a journey.

I was a worker bee carrying out my assigned tasks. I was physically present and active, but emotionally, I was dead. I did my work, went home, passed the time with meaningless distractions, ate, slept, and went back to work. Wash, rinse, repeat.

That didn't go well for me. I was successful in business but not in life. My relationships were a mess. I'd come home exhausted and wiped out. I wasn't eating or sleeping well. There was no passion in my life because passion needs to be felt deeply, and I just didn't have time for deep feelings.

But one emotion was getting through—depression—and I needed to insulate myself from that feeling. This world is full of distractions to indulge in, and I passed my time doing things that had no importance other than getting me through another day.

Then Mia happened.

The moment my daughter was born, my life changed. As I looked at my baby, time stood still. Every emotion I had bottled up over the years exploded inside me—as I held her, I was struck by a sense of wonder and awe I hadn't felt in years, and I was laughing, crying, and shaking all at once. She was perfect.

That moment was a turning point. I promised myself I'd be the best dad for Mia, and to do that, I had to embrace my emotions and stop living my life on autopilot. My daughter gave me the courage to take back the controls.

From Black & White to Living in Full Color

I recently heard a story about a man trying EnChroma glasses for the first time. One beautiful summer day, this man stood in his front yard with his family, and balloons of every color rested on the ground next to him. In his hands, he held a gift that was about to change his life—a pair of EnChroma glasses, a unique pair of lenses that allow colorblind people to perceive color.

For this man's entire life, his world was colorless, painted only in shades of gray. Before putting the glasses on, he said into the camera, "I have gone 65 years without seeing color. I am *not* going to get emotional."

Everyone around him stood still, waiting in anticipation for his reaction. After putting on the glasses, he stared at the trees and houses around him as if seeing them for the very first time. His son asked, "Is it totally different?"

Speechless, he put his hand over his mouth, but a sob burst through. He looked down. The balloons captured his attention next, and he let out another sob, overwhelmed by the explosion of color he could now perceive. All he could do was cry and hug his wife.

When people see color for the first time, their reactions are remarkably similar. They laugh, cry, or sit in stunned silence as they take in this new experience. It's more than about seeing color—it's about feeling, experiencing, and embracing a whole new dimension, a whole new world. It's overwhelming and emotional—and absolutely beautiful.

That's how I felt when I decided to reconnect with my emotions and own all of who I was—the good, the bad, and the ugly. I had stifled my feelings and emotions for so long that I didn't even know who I was anymore.

My world was colorless.

I had become a stranger to myself, caught up in the relentless pursuit of achievements and expectations, all while my true self remained hidden in the shadows.

But when I reconnected with my feelings and emotions, it was like putting on those glasses. A whole new dimension opened up in my life. My world, once flat and devoid of passion, was now filled with the rich, vibrant colors of joy, sorrow, and everything in between.

My emotional reawakening was beautiful and scary and over-whelming, but it was a precious gift that has reshaped my life in ways I couldn't imagine, and I'll never go back.

My life, once a dull gray, now bursts with color. With my emotions reawakened, I find joy in everything—relationships, nature, and the beauty in the simplest things. I learned to stay in the moment, to soak in life's wonders.

Now, years into my journey, life feels like being a kid in a candy store. I'm truly alive, and every day is a chance to experience something incredible. Being present means feeling everything deeply and meaningfully, and that's exactly what I try to do every day.

Passion Gave Way to Productivity

Like most kids, I was once fearless and full of passion. But I grew up in an environment where feelings weren't important—in fact, they were viewed more as a curse than a blessing. Success and results were what mattered most. Emotions were only unwanted distractions.

That's what most of the world focuses on now. If you want to feel important, you have to race frantically to the next big business or life goal. You have to surround yourself with "winners" who will help you get to the next level, and you need to "manifest" your next success, your next car, your fabulous new life. You have to drive yourself hard until you get there—wherever "there" is.

There's nothing wrong with having goals and working toward them, but when it gets out of balance and we only value results, we sacrifice our emotions and relationships on the altar of success. We start to view people around us as either assets or liabilities, and we monetize the people we care about.

Our focus turns from experience and joy to production. Other people become workers in our lives. It's all just a transaction. Will they help us reach our next milestone, or do we need to distance ourselves from them because they will slow us down?

When your worth is tied solely to your achievements, you're only as good as your latest success. Anyone can devalue you because your identity hinges on external validation instead of intrinsic worth.

When you live long enough like that, life gets drained of its color, and you don't even realize that you're living in a world filled with shades of gray. There's no depth, no fullness. Your accomplishments may be abundant, but if you don't engage with life on a more holistic level, deep feelings like joy and contentment are much harder to come by.

I fell into this trap. I worked for my father, and he saw my emotions as a problem, a weakness. I was much more manageable and could get more predictable results if I just worked harder. The only thing that mattered was getting results in business, and slowly but surely, my identity became intertwined with accolades and achievements, leading me on an endless quest for external validation.

However, I was on the edge of rediscovery, shifting from an ego-driven existence to a soul-driven life. Anchoring my identity to my soul allowed me to live authentically, guided by what truly brought me joy and fulfillment.

One of my mentors, Don, played a pivotal role in this transformation. Even though other people only saw me as a tool to get things done, he believed in me as a person. I loved to solve problems, and by putting me in situations where I would have to use my natural curiosity and drive, he helped to rebuild my self-confidence and reignite my passion.

Then, the birth of my daughter marked the definitive turning point, reintroducing vibrant color into my black-and-white world.

Have you ever heard of the butterfly effect? It's an idea that the world is so interconnected that even a tiny thing could influence a much larger system. Theoretically, a small butterfly flapping its wings could affect the weather and eventually cause a typhoon.

Well, when my daughter was born, I experienced the "Mia effect," and that tiny little creature changed the entire course of my life. Experiencing the profound and explosive emotions of fatherhood opened my eyes to the wonders of life that I had been missing, forever altering my perspective.

Open Your Emotional Toolbox

We all come into this world with an emotional toolbox equipped with many different feelings: passion, love, adoration, amusement, awe, desire, and even anger, confusion, disappointment, fear, and sadness. These emotions add depth, texture, and color to our lives. They enable us to connect deeply with others, touching our hearts and souls.

Without embracing these emotions, we risk living in shades of gray instead of vibrant hues. Life is meant to be lived up close in all its colorful, messy glory, not from a distance, insulated from our emotions.

Slipping into a monochrome existence can happen very subtly. We might start by distancing ourselves from our emotions, far from the vivid experiences we're capable of. Often, the fear of being over-whelmed, of losing our power or control, of being judged, or of getting hurt can lead us to shut down emotionally.

The modern world, with its constant digital connections and pressure to meet societal expectations, only amplifies this tendency. The endless stream of information and the need to please an ever-widening audience can leave us feeling like we'll never be enough, never do enough.

Unless we intentionally step away from that noise, the flood of information coming our way never stops. It's easy to get lost. We don't have time to process our emotions anymore. To cope, we mute our feelings and build walls. We numb ourselves out, or we pick up the tool of fear as a way to protect ourselves.

Fear is a natural defense mechanism, signaling danger and helping us avoid harm. However, relying on fear as our go-to emotional tool limits us. And if all of our other emotions continually get shut down, fear can creep in and take over every aspect of our lives.

Fear is one of the biggest enemies of a Satisfied Life.

Fear is just a mask for us to hide behind, but there's no satisfaction in that hiding place. So we seek refuge in distractions—anything from substance abuse to endless gaming to excessive spending—to momentarily escape and find comfort. Such diversions may seem tempting, offering quick gratification, but they can result in a disconnected existence. You end up sitting on the sidelines of your own life.

Fear of failure, heartache, and what other people think of us are three of the biggest deterrents to living our best lives. It makes us distance ourselves from others and even our own feelings. When we live with those fears long enough, they become our constant companions, and we get used to hiding.

Hiding in the Darkness

Stepping out of the shadows feels riskier than staying hidden, doesn't it? It's hard to walk in the sunlight where everything about you is crystal clear and magnified for the world to see.

As I'm sitting here, I'm looking at a palm tree under the bright sun. I notice the various shades of green on each leaf, but as the day moves into night, the different shades of green will disappear into a single dark shade.

That's how life can be. We can choose to linger in the fear-induced shadows, or we can step boldly into the richness life offers. Do we prefer to see the world through a limited, monochrome lens, where the shades of gray will deaden our engagement with the world? Or are we going to embrace life's vivid colors?

Fear, when used as our only guide, restricts us from profound experiences in life. And most of our fear isn't even real to begin with!

We terrify ourselves with the "what ifs," paralyzing our steps before we even begin. A life dominated by fear is only a half-life. Fear was never intended to be the master key in our emotional toolkit.

Let's step out of the dark shadows of uncertainty and embrace the full spectrum of our emotions. Life is far too precious to be experienced in anything less than its full, vivid spectrum. Choosing to live fully means diving headfirst into a sea of experiences and feeling every bit of it. It means feeling every emotion deeply and allowing ourselves to be moved by them.

The Strength of Our Emotions

Diving headfirst into the present and letting our emotions fill our lives doesn't make us fragile; it makes us more powerful. Yes, it can be intimidating because we want to appear strong, and we believe that showing any vulnerability will reveal our weaknesses and insecurities. But this couldn't be further from the truth. The deeper our connection with our emotions, the more unshakeable we become.

When we are genuinely the best version of ourselves, the opinions of others don't hold much power, and fear loses some of its influence. Instead, we become our own source of power.

Emotional awareness allows us to feel, listen, reflect, and act with conviction. It protects us from living a life of regret. Life doesn't wait. Moments will pass, with or without our consent. There's no pause or rewind button, so the best we can do is live in harmony with our feelings, making the most of every moment without being paralyzed by the "what-ifs."

The journey from the mind to the heart should be the shortest there is, yet we often make it one of the longest distances. But one of the greatest benefits of having a full spectrum of emotions at your disposal is the ability to live genuinely.

There is so much peace when you live in alignment with your soul. Listen deeply and reflect. Allow yourself to fully experience life— the good, the bad, and everything in between. Put in the effort to genuinely connect with others. Learn to find humor in your own mistakes and savor life's pleasures. You are stronger and more resilient than you realize.

PRACTICAL TIPS TO UNLOCK THE SATISFIED LIFE

Tell yourself the truth.

It can be hard to confront reality and acknowledge parts of yourself you may not be proud of or comfortable with. A decision to live authentically urges you to peel away society's expectations to discover your true self. The journey starts with self-awareness, recognizing your strengths and areas for growth. It's not an easy process, but growth and peace come along as part of the package.

Slow down.

Our modern lives are fast-paced and filled with distractions that can prevent us from connecting with our inner selves. Taking the time to slow down, even if it's just for a few moments each day, can help us tune into our thoughts and feelings. It's important to find peace in the present moment.

Get out into nature.

Nature has a unique way of putting things into perspective. Nature operates at a different pace—a slower rhythm compared to our hectic lives. Spending time in nature, like walking in the park, hiking in the mountains, or simply sitting by a body of water, can be incredibly grounding. It reminds us that we are part of something bigger, encouraging us to slow down and connect with the world around us.

Turn down the fear.

Fear of judgment or failure often holds us back from living our truth and expressing our emotions. What's the worst thing that's going to happen? Someone might not like you? There are over 8 billion people on this planet. No matter what you do, some people will love you, and some people will *never* like you. Accepting that is liberating. It allows you to live authentically, make mistakes, and grow from them. Every mistake is an opportunity to learn and evolve into the person you want to be.

Embrace your emotions.

Suppressing emotions is unhealthy and unsustainable. Like a ticking time bomb, bottled-up feelings will eventually explode, often at the wrong time and in front of the wrong people. Allow yourself to feel and process each emotion you have.

Wrap-Up and Next Steps

Locking away your emotions can make the world seem devoid of its true colors, leaving you in a landscape painted in nothing but black, white, and gray. Yet, by welcoming your emotions into your life, you unlock a full spectrum of vibrant colors—a richness and connection that comes only from accepting every part of yourself, including your emotions and feelings.

Understanding who you are and what brings you joy grants you power. Navigating life's challenges with resilience liberates you, making you truly powerful. The ability to feel deeply and express yourself without restraint connects you intimately to the world around you.

Are you truly present? Are you fully participating in the human experience in ways that enrich both your life and those of others? Or are you merely existing, filling time and space without purpose?

My journey to truly feeling alive didn't happen overnight. It required nurturing, acceptance, and the courage to let my emotions flow freely. I learned to live authentically, reclaiming my emotional vibrancy and embracing my true self.

This can be your story, too.

Take a moment to reflect. Look in the mirror ... really look. Now, allow yourself to feel whatever rises to the surface. Do you love the person looking back at you? Are you living freely and passionately? Does your life nourish your soul, or are you drifting, living by someone else's standards? Is your world bursting with color, or is it a dull expanse of gray?

If you find yourself feeling disconnected, numb, or adrift, know that it's not too late. Your world can burst into full color, starting right now. It's possible to embrace yourself for exactly who you are. To celebrate your strengths and unconditionally accept your flaws. To allow yourself to acknowledge what makes you feel good and pursue those things. To love deeply, let go of fear, and embrace life with courage, knowing you're living true to yourself.

What kind of person do you want to be? What is it that you, and you alone, want to do? Instead of letting others make choices for you along your journey, you can choose your own path. You have the power to take back control.

I want to invite you …

To be authentic and genuine with yourself. To be fully present, vulnerable, and strong. To live truthfully, nourishing your soul. To reconnect with nature, slow down, and reflect on your true self and life. To deepen your connections and soak up everything you can from even the most casual encounters throughout your day. To care profoundly and live with your whole heart.

To live a full-color life.

CHAPTER 2

RESPECT COMES EASY WHEN YOU KNOW YOUR WORTH

"Above all, don't lie to yourself. The man who lies to himself and listens to his own lie comes to a point that he cannot distinguish the truth within him, or around him, and so loses all respect for himself and for others. And having no respect, he ceases to love."

—FYODOR DOSTOEVSKY, *THE BROTHERS KARAMAZOV*

"What's the matter with you? Don't you know who I am?"

That was me—full of bravado, trying to convince myself and others that I was important and worthy of respect. I didn't realize that my behavior was a flashing sign of my emotional brokenness.

In my younger years, I didn't understand what respect truly meant. It was tied to either my performance or whatever power I thought I had. *Look at all the money you have—you must be worthy of respect.*

Look at all the people you know or all the parties you can get me into—you must be someone really special. Look at how you command other people's attention and respect—that power deserves respect.

During that time, I had no sense of my own worth. My value was wrapped up in my achievements and possessions, not in my identity as Alex. I felt compelled to fill my life with "success" and material possessions, hoping they would earn me the respect I craved. I wore these things like a coat of armor.

In a way, it was as if I was trying to buy respect.

Look around, and you'll see it everywhere: *I'm in the President's Club. I'm a top-tier level customer. Look at the car I'm driving. Look at how many followers I have on social media.*

When you have healthy self-respect, all those things are just perks in life. But if you're dealing with unresolved emotional issues, they become tools for seeking attention and validation, distractions from a deep-seated unhappiness.

VIP memberships are great for this. Being a Diamond Club member or carrying Elite status often brings special treatment and a sense of importance. Employees would thank me for my loyalty and give me extra attention to make me feel special so I would spend more money. It wasn't about me as a human. It was about what I could offer transactionally.

Relying on these surface relationships for validation made me feel good in the moment, but they gave me a false sense of worth. They ended up becoming distractions that prevented me from confronting my underlying issues.

The problem is that if you're buying respect, you can lose it. All those external markers of success can disappear, leaving you chasing the next accomplishment, making the next purchase, or throwing money around for attention.

I can look back at my younger self and see that I used to try to force people to respect me by looking and acting powerful. If someone denied me something I wanted, I would think, "Do you know who I am? You don't want to mess with me." I tried to be the tough guy. My sports cars and clothing were carefully chosen to impress others.

But I didn't like myself, and I was building up a lot of emotional debt because I wasn't respecting the moral code in my body. I wasn't listening to the voice inside of me telling me to do the right thing. If I did, I would then have to face the truth that I was living behind a facade and had lost touch with who I really wanted to be.

Focusing on VIP status and wealth was much easier than facing those uncomfortable truths. It was simpler to pretend everything was fine, but my unhappiness was lurking just under the surface, and the moment it was triggered, I'd come out fighting.

I was "successful" by society's standards, yet deeply unhappy. Not knowing how to fix myself, I lashed out, treating others poorly to feel powerful in the moment. It was easier to bring others down to my level than to confront my own life and unhappiness.

Respect Starts from Within

That started to change when two mentors came into my life and set me on a journey of genuine respect. These men offered a different perspective simply by modeling respect. They didn't want anything from me; they just wanted me to be a part of their lives. The feeling of validation and unconditional respect was transformative.

Their respect made me feel safe and gave me the freedom to set aside my insecurities and take a long, hard look at my life—who I was, who I wanted to be, and what truly made me happy or unhappy. As I began to understand what respect really was, I finally learned to respect myself and to honor my truth in every situation.

While my mentors set me on this path, it was my daughter who gave me the courage to confront the unprocessed emotions I had been avoiding for so long. She empowered me to face it head-on and start living authentically. It was a lot of work, but I wouldn't trade a moment of it because it has brought me peace and happiness.

This journey felt incredibly rewarding. By trusting my feelings and thoughts, I created a sense of safety within myself. Committing to self-respect allowed me to feel content in my body and environment, and I started taking care of myself physically and mentally.

I realized that respect can't be bought—it must be earned. I had to start with myself, and I had to do the work. The reward was huge! I discovered that when you start respecting yourself for who you are, that kind of respect can't be taken away.

This newfound respect began to radiate outward. You can't give what you don't already have. When I was unhappy, that negativity was all I could share. But as I addressed my emotional issues and started respecting myself, I became free to give out that respect to others.

I began to see the intrinsic value in others, not for what they could do for me, but for who they were. I felt grateful for the people in my life and wanted them to know it. I tried to make even casual acquaintances feel good by treating them well. It felt good to inject happiness and humor into those around me.

Respect Yourself First

Respect starts with you. The foundation of any form of respect begins with self-respect, both physically and mentally. If you can't respect yourself, it's impossible to extend it to others. And if you don't respect yourself, others will sense that and are less likely to respect you.

Our society often encourages us to disrespect ourselves. We sacrifice sleep. We indulge in harmful habits like drug use, excessive drinking, and other vices. We fail to manage the stress in our lives. In the name of convenience, we consume highly processed frankenfoods, often while rushing out the door, driving, or zoning out in front of a screen.

Our work/life balance can become skewed, and we can allow others' expectations and opinions to shape our lives and determine our paths, pulling us further away from our true selves. They dismiss our struggles with a simple, "You'll be fine."

My mentor, Don, gave me a valuable piece of advice: "Alex, your number one job is to not hurt Alex." At first, I didn't completely understand what that meant, but as I focused more on self-care, the importance of this advice became clear. It was all about self-respect.

Self-care profoundly impacts how we show up in the world, how we make decisions, and how others perceive us. When we take care of ourselves, we are calmer and more present. We make better decisions—less impulsivity and fewer knee-jerk reactions to those around us. Being able to take a breath and respond differently to disrespect saves us from grief and regret.

On the other hand, neglecting self-care clouds our judgment. We lack the energy to handle unnecessary drama and find it challenging to treat others respectfully. Our focus turns inward, affecting our ability to empathize and connect with others.

So, How's That Working Out for You?

Whenever I talked through some of my poor decisions with a therapist, she would always ask, "How's that working out for you?" I hated that question, but it always led to profound insights. To this day, this question helps me quickly get back on track.

Try it yourself. Think of an action you took that didn't align with your moral code. It could have been about the way you were you were treated. It could have been about the way you treated yourself. It could have been about how you treated others or even your environment and possessions.

Replay that scenario in your mind, then honestly ask yourself, *how's this working out for me?*

When I was younger, my lifestyle seemed fun for a while, but in reality, it was lonely. I didn't feel good. I was losing weight and living recklessly, with no regard for the value of life. So how was it working out for me? The truth was, it wasn't working out well at all. I was masking my unhappiness and running from my problems.

In order to start living according to my truth, I needed control and a sense of safety. The only way to achieve that was to simplify my life and focus on what I could control—immersing myself in nature, changing my diet, getting enough sleep, and carefully choosing who I allowed into my life. And I had to always tell myself the truth. The other variables were out of my control. That's how I began my journey of self-respect.

Without self-respect, you can't truly respect others. You must love yourself unconditionally and care for yourself enough to express that love. If you can't do that, how can you connect meaningfully with anyone else?

Respect Costs Zero Dollars

At the end of the day, we all just want to feel like we matter. We crave care, recognition, and the feeling of being seen and heard.

When I encounter disrespectful people, I remind myself that there's often a deeper reason behind their behavior. They might be facing health scares, financial struggles, job pressures, or intense anxiety. Perhaps they feel inadequate or disrespected. There's usually an underlying issue behind bad behavior.

I've learned that I have the power to change their day for the better, and it feels like a superpower. When you honor someone by unconditionally validating them—truly listening and engaging with them and treating them as the remarkable individuals they are—it's like injecting a dose of love and happiness into their lives. And the good feelings go both ways; this act of respect makes my life richer, filled with gratitude and delight.

Respect has the power to forge deep connections and friendships. When you genuinely value people, you'd be surprised at the doors that open for you, the unexpected gifts that come your way, and the beautiful relationships that grow out of it.

There's absolutely no downside to respect. And the best part? It's free.

Respect as a Gauge

Before we step outside, we can check a weather app to know what kind of day to expect. The temperature and rain chances guide us on how to dress and prepare.

Similarly, respect serves as a gauge to measure our emotional and spiritual health. The level of respect or disrespect we show to ourselves and others indicates whether we are emotionally sound or carrying unresolved emotional issues.

If someone is deeply unhappy or lacks validation, certain situations will trigger them, highlighting their unhappiness. They then face a choice: confront the underlying issue that needs healing or divert their negativity onto something else to avoid the real problem.

Being easily triggered and lashing out is a clear sign that someone is carrying emotional debt, which keeps them off balance. Show me a disrespectful person, and I'll show you someone with unprocessed or ignored emotions.

I saw this in my own life. Whenever I overreacted or lashed out over feeling inconvenienced or disrespected, I realized I was projecting past issues onto others due to unresolved emotional debt.

Snapping at somebody usually requires less emotional energy than looking inward and finding the wounded part of our souls. But covering up our unhappiness and disrespecting others is damaging, building walls in our relationships and ultimately making us even more unhappy.

Triggers highlight areas that need healing, and that's good news! Now, when I feel the urge to lash out, I take a different approach. First, I stay silent and count until the frustration subsides. Once the moment passes, I examine the situation with curiosity—what was really going on? What emotion or memory was triggered that still needs healing? I confront it directly and deal with it. It takes effort, but it's worth it because I refuse to let unprocessed emotions control me.

Whether by journaling, talking it out, or seeking professional help, it's crucial to slow down and address these areas. Ignoring them keeps you imprisoned, but dealing with them sets you free.

PRACTICAL TIPS TO UNLOCK THE SATISFIED LIFE

Take care of yourself.
When you're healthy and taking care of yourself, you present the best version of yourself. People are drawn to those who are healthy, caring, and strong.

Don't lose sight of your own life goals.
If you're not focused on your own agenda and self-care, other people's agendas can creep in, slowly replacing what you know to be best for you. Always keep your best self and your goals at the forefront.

Slow down.
We often go a thousand miles an hour, but respect requires connection, and connection requires quality time.

Stay away from the "Ds."
Disrespect, disengagement, disruption, depression, drugs, and dumbasses—they all feed into a downward spiral, trapping you. Recognize when these negative elements start to creep in and consciously change direction.

Get to know someone's journey.

Make a conscious effort to see the individual and listen more than you speak. When you are fully engaged and emotionally present, people will connect with you because they feel seen and heard.

Focus on what you have in common with someone.

We often only see snapshots of a person's life. By taking time to see the goodness in someone and finding common ground, you can significantly improve even casual encounters.

Acknowledge and validate.

Letting someone know you appreciate or care about them can have a huge impact. They'll remember you because not many people take the time to do this. Strive to leave people better than you found them.

Practice restraint, not reaction.

Thomas Jefferson once advised, "When angry, count ten before you speak; if very angry, a hundred." Reacting poorly when triggered is human, but it often leaves everyone feeling worse. Instead, take a breath, count to ten, and then count again if needed. Let the emotions subside before responding.

To shut down a verbal attack, just say, "Ouch!"

If someone is verbally attacking you, saying "Ouch" can effectively stop the attack because there's not much to say in response to that. It disrupts the aggression and allows you to redirect the conversation.

Pay attention to your triggers.

If you find yourself angrier than you should be, use that moment to slow down and reflect on the cause. Identify any unresolved trauma or issues that may have led to this reaction, and seek healing for past hurts.

Know when to walk away.

If someone is determined to make poor choices, it's not your responsibility to change them. Reach out if you can, but if they're not receptive, it's wise to step back. Wish them well and move on.

Wrap-Up and Next Steps

If you recognize some patterns of disrespect and unhappiness in your own life after reading this chapter, now is a good time to address those patterns. Remember, they didn't develop overnight and won't be fixed overnight. Improvement is a journey, not a quick fix, but you can make progress, even if it's just a small step each day.

Start by telling yourself the truth. No one else's truth can fill the void created by ignoring your own. Respect isn't something you can buy—it must be earned. It begins with self-respect and doing the necessary work. The reward is immense! When you respect yourself for who you are, that respect becomes a part of you.

Set aside the mindset of disrespect and return to what genuinely makes you feel good. Start with small pleasures. It might feel unfamiliar at first, given how long you've been conditioned not to feel good. But give it a try. Find something simple that brings you joy, and allow yourself to enjoy that feeling. Eventually, feeling good becomes contagious and infectious—you'll crave it all the time.

You'll start to notice when you step out of this place of contentment. By slowing down and adjusting your perspective, attitude, and behavior, respect will become your dominant pattern. Over time, respect for yourself and for others will seamlessly integrate into your daily life.

I want to invite you …

To pause and take a deep look at your life. To set aside any regret or shame and to look instead through the lens of curiosity. To examine those triggering moments, uncover what's hiding behind them, and then deal with them and get free.

To set aside everyone else's agenda and pick up your own, caring for your body, mind, and spirit. To confront your issues and heal from past traumas. To tell yourself the truth about your life—especially in areas where you fall short. To identify one area where you can heal and move the needle forward.

To reconnect with a time when you felt amazing and resume from there, charting a new course filled with respect and gratitude. When faced with disrespect, to walk away and wish the person well. To treat others kindly, even when it's undeserved. To strive to leave people better than you found them.

To honor and appreciate your life, to cherish every day, to value your experiences, and to live without regrets.

CHAPTER 3

PROTECT YOUR ENERGY

"The most important things in life are your
connections to other people."

—TOM FORD

Living in touch with my emotions meant opening myself up to some painful times too. My ex was not in a place where she could provide the best upbringing for our daughter, so from the tender age of two weeks until she turned 16, I fought tirelessly for custody. The battle wore me down, but I refused to quit.

Mia's mom accused me of doing things I didn't do, and there were moments when even my own family, with the exception of my mother, turned their backs on me and sided with my ex. It was a heartbreaking experience. All I wanted was to protect my daughter and shower her with unconditional love.

I remember one specific day when I walked into the courthouse for yet another grueling appearance, feeling utterly defeated. I was tired. My head hung low, my eyes fixated on the ground beneath me. I had reached a point where I was just so over it all.

My lawyer, John York, wasn't a mudslinger—he only focused on facts and the truth. John stopped me in my tracks. He looked me in the eyes and said, "Did you do the things your ex is accusing you of doing?"

I said, "No, I did not."

He said, "Then quit buying into her agenda. What is the truth? The truth is that you're a dad who wants to take care of his daughter. Focus on who you are. Wear the white hat. Hold your head up high when you go in there because this is who you are. You're a dad, and no one can take that away from you."

He was right. I was doing the right thing. Both the court and an independent psychologist had determined that I was the better parent for my daughter, and I was fighting a noble fight. John urged me to look beyond my immediate struggles and see the good that still existed within those courthouse walls. People were celebrating adoptions, and families were reconnecting there. He told me to take a moment and be grateful for all the positive things happening amidst the chaos. And so, I did. I picked my head up and stood tall.

That simple act changed everything. It shifted my perspective, reinvigorated my energy, and reignited the fire within me. The battle was far from over, but on that day, I learned some invaluable lessons.

I discovered that I was strong and knew how to stay true to myself, even in adversity. I realized that attitude is everything, and it can transform every situation. I learned that even in the darkest moments, goodness and light still exist. I understood that my life was worth living, even when things weren't going my way.

I was rewarded with peace and fulfillment. And today, my daughter and I share a bond that most people can only dream of.

Manage Your Energy, Not Your Time

Part of bringing the best of yourself to the world involves managing your time and energy. There are so many books out there about time management that I don't want to focus on it. Instead, I like to focus on energy management.

Energy management focuses on how you handle your priorities. For instance, if your child has a recital one evening, but you find yourself too tired to go, is that about time management or energy management? I argue that it's about energy management. If you've spent all of your energy at work and when you come home, you either can't or don't want to actively work on your relationships, you're out of balance and not managing your energy well.

I like to view energy as currency—as "energy credits."

We only have a set amount of time, but that's not necessarily true for energy. Spending time with chaotic people who are steeped in negativity and constantly complaining will suck the energy out of you. It's like making a bad investment, depleting these precious credits. Our energy drains away at an accelerated pace, and we can drain even more of our energy by complaining or fault-finding. That emotional drain may not leave enough positive energy to affect the people we love.

But unlike time that relentlessly slips away, energy can be renewed and replenished. Some relationships and activities can invigorate and strengthen us, giving us more energy credits to spend in a day.

Manage your energy. Allocate your time. Time isn't something you can control, but you can actively refill your energy reserves by focusing on your most important priorities: seeking out the beauty in your life, sleeping well, taking care of yourself, and spending time with positive people.

Not long ago, I received some beautiful messages from people letting me know that I had helped them and had a positive impact on them. One day, when I was feeling down, I reread the messages, and my energy and mood instantly improved. How could I feel bad after reading those notes? I added energy credits just by reconnecting with positive people and allowing the gratitude and wonderful feelings to replenish me.

Take a moment to reflect on how you've been nurturing yourself mentally and emotionally. Are you trying to live up to others' expectations of who you should be and how you should live? Are you in a relentless pursuit of "success"? It's easy to pour all our energy, creativity, and emotional capacity into our work, leaving little room for what's most important. Too often, by the time we get home, our tanks are practically empty, and we try to run our personal lives and relationships on fumes.

But what if we made a simple switch from work/life balance to life/work balance? At first glance, it sounds trivial, but think about this for a moment. Instead of making work your top priority, what if you prioritize your relationships over work? With that simple shift in focus, would your life have more balance? What would happen to your energy levels?

In an interview with Steven Bartlett on *The Diary of a CEO* podcast (December 7, 2023), relationship therapist Esther Perel said,

"Do you know a single person who would treat their business the way some people treat their relationships? The business would be dead. But the quality of your life is determined by the quality of your relationships."

Think about your relationships with the people most important to you. Are you bringing the best version of yourself, or do you have only leftovers for your loved ones? How about with people who even briefly come into your life? Do you have the energy to love with your whole heart?

It takes a conscious decision to give yourself and your relationships more than just the energy-depleted version of yourself. But if you make the choice, your relationships and even your everyday casual interactions will be catapulted to a different level of satisfaction.

Time Vs. Things

One reason why social media can be so addictive is that we often get run-down and have no emotional energy left, and social media lets us check out of life for a bit. So we pick up our phones and become emotional zombies, scrolling through social media, getting a dopamine hit without expending much energy. We can just hit a button—we don't have to engage with that other person. That dopamine hit feels good in the short term, but in the long term, we pay a price in our relationships.

Even though we feel better in the moment, we don't gain any energy credits. We're not doing something that fills up our energy reservoirs. It doesn't help us show up any better in the world. We're feeling okay, but we're not putting good things back out into the world.

There are so many different ways to "check out" and get lost in mind-numbing activities that, in the end, won't improve the quality of your life. There's nothing wrong with a little bit of mindless activity, but guard your energy carefully because the time you give up will never be returned to you.

Time may slip away, but how you use it is up to you. You can impact this world by making those energy credits count!

PRACTICAL TIPS TO UNLOCK THE SATISFIED LIFE

Make relationships a priority, not an afterthought.
Relationships will wither and die if we don't put any effort or energy into them. Loving people well requires action.

Don't discount the small gestures.
Even the smallest act to show someone you care about them can change their day. Eye contact, a smile, and being present in even brief moments may not seem like much, but they can make a dramatic difference to someone who's having a rough day.

Be fearless.
Approaching others with curiosity and openness disarms them and helps them relax. Fear of rejection shouldn't be a barrier. Remember, rejection isn't a reflection of your worth.

Be present.
Let people know they are important by shutting off distractions and giving them all of your focus and presence. Be an active listener—engage with what they're saying.

Make people feel welcome.

Say cheese! A genuine smile is a simple gesture of kindness that costs nothing but can mean everything. Show respect, make them laugh, and leave them feeling better for having met you.

Make the interaction about them, not about you.

It's easy to focus all of our energy on impressing people. We worry about how they see us, and trying to impress people can be exhausting. But if we can stop comparing ourselves and just respect the other person as a human being, it allows us to stop measuring ourselves against each other and instead open up a genuine conversation. Now, we can talk from the heart.

Seek and highlight the positive.

Society often steers us toward criticism. Instead, identify and celebrate the positive traits in others. Find common ground based on the positives.

Let the past be the past.

If previous interactions have been rocky, let go and start afresh. Today is a new day. You have the power to choose how you want to communicate with someone.

Bond through stories.

Sharing real-life stories creates a powerful emotional bond. Authenticity in your experiences and emotions invites others to connect with that same depth within themselves.

Handle your "energy credits" wisely.

Complaining and negative thinking saps precious energy from you. Most of the time, it's just not worth it. Stop worrying about things you can't control or change. Focus instead on what you can do to preserve and build up your energy for the things that really matter in life.

Seek out people who renew your energy.

Maximize the interactions where both you and the other person feel safe and honored.

Identify the "energy vampires" in your life and limit your time with them.

Guard your energy carefully around the people who drain it from you. You can't avoid them entirely, but you can protect yourself just by being mindful of the people who drain your energy.

Wrap-Up and Next Steps

Managing your energy is one of the keys to living a Satisfied Life. What gives you energy? What drains it? If you pay attention to where your energy comes from, when it goes up, and when it dips, you'll know how to protect your energy.

Don't be afraid to let go of the energy vampires in your life. Distance yourself from them so you can use your energy to change your corner of the world.

At the same time, identify the people you want to take with you on your journey—the people who make you stronger by being with them, who take care of your heart.

Embrace even the tough parts of your life. Challenges, heartaches, and hurdles are essential chapters of your life's story, shaping you into the person you are today. Welcome the full spectrum of your experiences and relationships.

You are here for a reason. You are here to make a difference, leave the world a better place, and have a lasting impact. But without energy, how can you make a difference? It's essential to have a reserve of energy ready for when you need it most.

CHAPTER 4

HARNESS YOUR PASSION TO CREATE YOUR ROADMAP

"Passion is the bridge that takes you
from pain to change."

—FRIDA KAHLO

With my gym bag slung over my arm, ready for my daily workout, I made my way into the gym. It was buzzing with activity. The smell of sweat and metal and the unmistakable sound of clattering weights filled the room. But amid the movement and distraction, I couldn't help but notice one trainer, Chase, who radiated passion and energy.

It was also impossible not to notice that he had a prosthetic arm.

I never meet a stranger anymore, so I struck up a conversation with him when he was done working with his client. I wanted to know his story since it seemed clear that he was fully immersed in what he loved. In his world, nothing was beyond that moment with his client, but his enthusiasm radiated beyond their space and out into the room.

He told me he was born with only one arm and that kids in his neighborhood and at school were really cruel. He grew up carrying a chip on his shoulder, constantly asking himself, *Why me? Things would be so much better if I had two arms.* The resentment festered, and he wore his anger like a shield.

Despite having only one arm, Chase had a deep love for sports and a fiery determination to outshine everyone around him. He worked tirelessly, pushing himself harder than anyone else just to level the playing field, and he excelled in athletics.

But that resentment never left him, and as he grew older, it led him down a dark path of addiction and despair. His brothers also battled addiction, and the path filled with drugs and failure was always right in front of him. Finally, living out of his car, he began to look at his life with brutal honesty. That's when he had a moment of clarity.

At the end of his rope, he said he realized that anger, a victim mentality, and drugs weren't going to lead him anywhere good. "I had to snap out of it and find something I was truly passionate about, something that would give me purpose and set me on a better path."

Chase thought about the saying, "Do what you love, and you won't work a day in your life." As he mulled it over, he decided that sports and fitness were his passion—not as an athlete, but as a mentor. So, he began to educate himself. He redirected all of his passion and energy and poured it into the life he was envisioning as an MMA trainer.

Training others soon became his art, his calling, his obsession.

Years later, Chase feels alive, invigorated, and content. He said, "I feel so fulfilled. I'm helping my clients reach their goals, helping them develop according to their needs. I don't get tired of it. I still love it. I still get excited. And I'm making a difference in people's lives.

"I think too many people these days are stuck doing things they're not passionate about, and it leads to a dull, unfulfilled life. They end up trapped in a box, feeling like they're not making a real contribution or pursuing their true passions. Living that way for years on end, no wonder people feel depressed. They're not engaging with something that captures their souls, that sets their hearts on fire.

"But when you find something you're passionate about, life is rich. I get to share something I love with other people. I may not have the most money in the world, but in my soul, I'm rich. And I think that's why people are drawn to me. This is my passion, and it shines through in everything I do."

Passion Doesn't Disappear

We are created to feel deeply, to experience all of our emotions, and to live life fully. Our souls yearn for deep connection with others, nature, and the world in general. We are hard-wired for passion, fulfillment, and purpose.

However, this vibrant energy of passion and emotion does not simply vanish when we try to suppress or ignore it. If we attempt to bury our feelings or neglect our emotional well-being, that powerful energy will persist. And it will find its way to the surface, either physically or mentally.

In my own life, I can remember feeling like a robot when I was younger. I wasn't supposed to feel, just produce. I just had to focus on doing the next thing. But my emotions refused to be ignored. I was miserable, and that emotional energy found ways to seep out. I was often sick during the holidays when I had to stifle my feelings the most. I was frustrated and angry, and my anger spilled out on the people around me. I was a tough person to like at times.

But when I allowed all of that neglected energy and emotion to come up and drive me toward what I truly loved and wanted out of life, it transformed me. My hard heart began to soften up. I took responsibility for my life and thought about who I wanted to be and who I *didn't* want to be. And suddenly, it was like I had a roadmap for my life.

Just like my new friend Chase, I could see clearly where I was and the path I was on, and I wanted something different for my life. I realized I had the power to choose a new path. Once I started focusing on my passion and emotions, I became less reactive to the ugliness in the world. I felt a new zeal for life. My new route was filled with purpose, peace, and happiness.

Your Personal Map

If you take a trip to Disney World, a big mall, or a sprawling museum, you will usually find a large map that lays out the entire area. Prominently featured on this map is a red dot, a beacon declaring, "You Are Here."

No matter where you want to end up on that map, you must first understand where you are. The same is true when you navigate your journey of personal growth. Without acknowledging your starting point, the path toward your aspirations becomes a game of chance. But when you know your starting point, the most direct route to the life you want becomes clear.

Many personal development speakers emphasize the importance of focusing on your goals, on where you aim to be. And they're not wrong—having a clear vision for your future is necessary. It's what motivates you to push forward. However, I've met so many people who only know where they want to go. They haven't taken the time to figure out their starting point. "You Are Here" doesn't exist on their map.

No matter how big your dreams are, they remain out of reach if you're unclear about where your journey begins. Your starting point determines your direction.

What does your map look like? Along with your dreams, do you have a spot on your map marked "You Are Here"? Pinpointing your current location will help you plot the best course toward your goals.

First Step: Own Your Reality

First and foremost, you have to get honest with yourself. If you're not living a fulfilling life, emotionally debt-free, then you have made some choices that have led you to this point. Or maybe it was that you failed to make choices. Perhaps you failed to take control of your life, and you drifted away from happiness because you gave up your power to make decisions for yourself. Either way, you have to understand your current state in relation to the person you want to be.

You can't effectively imagine a different future without understanding where you've been and the experiences that have influenced you. Your past, with all its victories and setbacks, has shaped you into who you are, right here, right now, and your past can help you define the future you do—and do not—want.

Don't be afraid to give yourself a thorough life audit. What are the wins? What are the losses? What's preventing your happiness? If there's a recurring pattern of negativity, like choosing toxic relationships or continually losing your job, there's likely a root cause that needs uncovering. Own everything—the good and the bad.

Neutralize Negativity.

When you're examining your life, you will face some truths about yourself that aren't pleasant. But there's no room for shame or self-contempt. Understanding who you are is only a tool to get you to where you want to go, not a weapon to beat yourself up with.

If the idea of facing some of your harder truths feels overwhelming, try shifting your perspective. Detach yourself from your story for a moment and view your life as if it were someone else's. Observe without judgment. Learn. If a negative emotion arises, acknowledge it, feel it, and then let it go.

Your past does not define your future.

Yes, your past does influence your future, but its influence can be positive instead of negative. Owning your mistakes allows you to learn from them. They become lessons that highlight what you value most, guiding your desires for the future. You become a wiser and stronger version of yourself. And when you acknowledge your past and own it all, you receive the gift of peace. In the words of Marvin Gaye: "If you cannot find peace within yourself, you will never find it anywhere else."

Second Step: Dream Your Ideal Reality

In the story at the beginning of this chapter, Chase tapped into his passion. He figured out what he loved, what lit him up with energy, what made him feel like he was living a meaningful life. He allowed himself to envision a fulfilling life, free from anger, pain, and drug use. He focused on his goal to be a trainer, physically and psychologically helping others to be amazing MMA fighters.

Living out of his car, Chase faced his reality and firmly put down the "You Are Here" dot on the map of his life. It wasn't pretty, but he didn't make time for negative feelings and self-judgment. It was simply his starting point.

With a beginning and a destination in mind, Chase could clearly plot a course to get to his dreams.

His journey wasn't easy—most journeys aren't. My dad always says, "Who told you it would be easy? If it was easy, everyone would be doing it." But for those who do put in the effort to walk along that path to their dreams, the reward is a well-lived, satisfying life.

Third Step: Road Trip!

A route on any map is rarely a direct path. The road ahead will twist and turn. You'll encounter detours and reroutes, face heavy traffic, and navigate through construction zones. Stops for fuel, meals, and rest are not just interruptions; they're integral parts of the journey.

Similarly, the emotional route from your current state to your desired future won't follow a straight line. Mistakes will be made. Distractions will arise, and you may sometimes revert to familiar destructive patterns. Your journey will be marked by starts and stops, detours, and moments for rest and reflection.

Your journey will not be perfect. And that's okay! Your greatest lessons can be learned by doing life imperfectly.

Embrace the imperfection of your journey. It's completely normal not to get everything right. Acceptance and peace will accompany you, not because you're flawless, but because you're on the right path. Just pivot and continue forward.

Let your personal roadmap guide you toward the life you yearn for. Allow your passions to lead the way, and watch for the signs of peace, joy, and gratitude along the road. And don't forget to cherish the journey itself, not just the destination.

PRACTICAL TIPS TO UNLOCK THE SATISFIED LIFE

Tell yourself the truth.

Don't be afraid to identify where your life may be going astray. Own those aspects and turn them to your advantage. Use them to help you figure out what you want your life to look like.

Spend your energy on your roadmap.

The more you focus on the good that is all around you, the more enjoyable your journey will be. Instead of getting caught up in other people's drama, fill your days with positive people and experiences.

Take small steps if you need to.

Change is a process, not an overnight transformation. Begin with small steps, addressing one aspect of your emotional burden at a time, allowing each positive change to build on the last.

Don't play the blame game.

Even when pointing fingers at someone feels justified, there's a downside to the blame game—you give your power away to the other person or the situation. Someone or something else has control over your happiness, over your life. But you are a survivor, not a victim.

Change your perspective.

With every challenge lies an opportunity for growth. Focus on the positives, and actively replace negative thoughts with constructive ones. Over time, this habit will become a way of life.

Let go of your pain and negative feelings.

Recognize any negative feelings or pain you've been holding onto, and then release them. They belong in the past. Today is a new day.

Celebrate your wins.

Good comes out of even our biggest mistakes. Learn, grow, leave the negative in the past, and carry the positive into your future.

Wrap-Up and Next Steps

Living a satisfying, fulfilling life, full of passion and joy, isn't something you just stumble into. You have to choose your life and take control of your destiny. You have to be intentional and own the day, every day.

This requires asking yourself some tough questions. Where do you stand now, and where do you aspire to be? If there's a gap, if you've strayed from your intended path, it's crucial to acknowledge your current state and get back on the course that resonates with your core being.

It's not always easy, but you are up to the task. Your walk along the path of being emotionally debt-free will not be perfect, but it doesn't have to be. Imperfection is part of the process. Embrace your strengths and weaknesses. Look at everything you are and own all of it.

Consider this your permission slip to ask all the challenging questions, free from disappointment or shame. To scrutinize your life with honesty, embracing every part of it. To love and accept yourself unconditionally. To own all of who you are—both the good and the bad. To acknowledge your past, your missteps, and your negative emotions, then let them go.

To realign with what feeds your soul, to let passion guide you, infusing your life with wonder and gratitude. To embrace and enjoy your journey. To pivot away from the negative and toward the positive, and to seek out the good that accompanies every challenge.

To feel like a complete person once again. To seize the day and live an extraordinary life.

CHAPTER 5

THE POWER OF DEEP CONNECTION

"Connection is the energy that exists between people
when they feel seen, heard, and valued; when they can
give and receive without judgment."

—BRENÉ BROWN

On a day that should have been filled with joy, my friend Katie was terrified. She went into the hospital to give birth to her first child, but what started out as a routine procedure spiraled into a life-threatening emergency.

Her baby became lodged in the birth canal, and an emergency C-section was not an option. In a matter of minutes, the delivery room morphed into a frenzied battle zone as medical teams worked to save both mother and child.

She found herself in the middle of a nightmare, wondering and silently pleading, *Are we going to die? Oh, God, please don't let us die.*

Katie lay there helpless, her body injured by the intense efforts to get the baby free and delivered. She was engulfed in pain. Her family, pushed to the edge of the room, could only watch in distress and pray. The chaos overwhelmed her. Physical pain mixed with fear and uncertainty, and she could barely breathe.

Her doctor was able to get her son through the birth canal, but he wasn't breathing. As the medical teams worked to resuscitate him and stabilize Katie, equipment alarms beeping and doctors frantically giving orders, she caught a glimpse of her mother praying in the corner of the room.

Her husband had made his way to her side, and she felt the warmth of his hand on her forehead. His prayers, gentle and reassuring, soothed her. His presence grounded her. He was an anchor in the storm.

Then her friend appeared on Katie's other side. She leaned over and whispered into Katie's ear, "I'm here!"

Miraculously, Katie and her child survived and are thriving today. But it took more than the skill of doctors and nurses. Katie needed the support and strength of her friends and family.

When she felt as if her whole world was about to crumble, she leaned on the strength and protection of those she could trust with her heart. In her most vulnerable moments, the people who mentally got her through the next hours, days, and ultimately, years, were those she had chosen to share her life with.

In the same way, when I realized I would be raising a child by myself, my mom was right there to support me and love both of us through years of heartache and pain, as well as inexplicable joy and lots of life's little pleasures. My mom was my safe haven when I was growing up. No matter how many times I stumbled or made mistakes, she listened to me without judgment. Everything was okay to talk about, and everything could be worked through.

This is why it's vital to surround ourselves with people who will stand by us, no matter what. At some point in our lives, we all need unwavering love and support. Like strands in a rope, each one of us is strong individually, but together, we form an almost unbreakable bond.

Unlike business achievements, which can be measured, the value of healthy relationships is beyond measure. Nurturing deep connections with each other creates a sense of safety and mutual trust. When we feel safe and loved, we're able to extend that same warmth and positivity to others. We radiate peace and joy. We feel empowered and fulfilled. And we know that we can overcome anything life throws our way.

Presence Creates Safety

Fortunately, most of us aren't usually in a moment of extreme crisis like Katie was. But in our everyday encounters, how often do we come upon people going through their own challenges that we don't know about? How many times do we cross paths with people who are feeling alone, helpless, afraid, or insignificant?

This is going to sound crazy, but I was at The Home Depot recently, and amidst the busy shoppers, I noticed a golden retriever lying peacefully on the floor. This scene—a dog peacefully resting in the middle of a busy store—drew me in.

I like to do unexpected things and shake people out of their mindless routines, so without another thought, I lay down beside him. The dog licked my hand while I gently petted him.

As I immersed myself in the moment, a simple yet profound realization dawned on me: I was meeting him at his level, both physically and metaphorically. As a result, I shared a beautiful moment with him, even in the middle of the chaos all around us.

That small act mirrors a larger truth we often miss in our interactions with others.

When someone around us is struggling, we don't often take the time to get on their level and see the world through their eyes. We're quick to offer solutions, to "fix" things, but how often do we choose to simply be there, to provide a space where they can express themselves freely, without fear of judgment or unsolicited advice?

By being curious and allowing ourselves to be a sounding board for someone, we can often let the other person potentially work out their situation. Usually, the answers are within them—they just need to be seen, heard, and understood in order to work it out.

It's in these unguarded moments that we find genuine beauty and connection. Each time you are truly present, you not only make your life richer, but you impact those around you in profound, often unseen ways.

By being present, by allowing yourself to be vulnerable and open, you invite others to do the same. By sharing your world, you make others feel safe enough to open up and share their world, and this mutual exchange of trust and understanding creates deep, meaningful connections. You become intertwined in each other's stories.

In our fast-paced world, we often become so focused on achieving goals, making money, and accomplishing tasks that we neglect the simple skill of connecting with each other.

I grew up in that kind of results-driven atmosphere, so naturally, I would approach people with questions like, *How can I fix this? And if I can't fix something and make their situation better, then what role do I play? What could I possibly do for them?* This mindset, however, led me to withdraw, especially when others needed genuine emotional support the most.

In relationships, trust becomes the currency, and time outweighs measurable results. Success in a relationship is often measured by simply being there for someone, providing a sense of safety, and making them feel valued on their life's journey alongside you.

Not even physical distance can diminish this feeling of safety. Take my daughter, for instance. She now lives across the country from me, walking out her own journey. She's not afraid to take on life because she knows beyond a shadow of a doubt that I am always there for her. I have her back, no matter what. She feels secure knowing that I am always a phone call away, and I will help her navigate past any obstacle she faces. Even when I'm not with her, I'm there for her unconditionally.

Making people feel safe works not just with our closest relationships but also with our everyday interactions. Whether it's a friend or just a casual acquaintance, being present for them, caring about them, and letting them into your life can make anyone feel safe and valued. That can bring even casual encounters to a whole different experience.

We All Crave Real Connection

Have you ever tried to carry on a conversation with someone while they are scrolling on their phone? They might be physically present, but their thoughts and emotions are split between two different worlds. Doesn't it almost feel like you're trying to talk to a wall? Your words aren't being heard. There's no real connection.

When you're only half there, it creates a feeling of loneliness for the person you are with. Being half-present sends a clear and rather rude message: something else is more important than you. Now, flip the script. When you genuinely acknowledge someone, it's powerful. Your actions are saying: *You matter. You're important.* It's a simple yet profound way to make a person feel special.

Imagine bonding with someone on a deeper level, where your eyes, your facial expressions, and your undivided attention do more than words ever could. It's not just about words; it's about the connection. This kind of connection breaks down walls of even complete strangers, creating space for them to open up to you.

Now more than ever, people are craving this kind of genuine connection. They want to be heard, to feel significant. They want to feel safe. They want to feel like they're a priority in your life, and that you are a priority in their life as well.

Creating a safe space is critical to making people feel secure. It's really about being human—engaging in genuine conversation, listening intently, and valuing what the other person has to share. People feel safe when they know they're being heard and their thoughts and feelings are respected without judgment. This kind of environment brings healing and allows them to embrace their fear and overcome it, becoming fearless.

It All Begins with You

You can't give what you don't have—you can only give what you already have yourself, so making others feel safe starts with you. Have you made your life a safe haven for yourself?

Bringing a feeling of safety and importance starts with developing a deep, comfortable relationship with yourself. You are a human with strengths, flaws, and insecurities. Can you own and accept every bit of it? Can you sit comfortably with who you are, without the urge to escape or distract yourself from your perceived shortcomings?

When you are at peace with who you are, you will feel free to express yourself, to be genuine and authentic with yourself and others. You become fearless.

The Magic of NOW

In our fast-moving world, the art of making genuine human connections often takes a back seat. But the true value of relationships isn't in wealth, social media followers, or fame, but in nurturing deep, unconditional, love-filled bonds.

We make people feel safe and valued by taking a moment to connect as human beings, giving them our undivided attention. That's not always easy to do. We often take great pride in being amazing multitaskers, able to handle the flood of information constantly coming at us.

Sometimes it seems that the world is moving so fast around us. Social media, commercials, and "influencers" loudly demand what we are supposed to think, feel, and do. It's easy to lose sight of the here and now. But being present, truly present, is a gift you can give yourself and those around you, and it's FREE. It's about more than just showing up physically in a place; it's about immersing yourself fully in the moments that make up your life.

If you started living each moment as if the next doesn't exist, how would your day be different?

There's a certain magic in embracing the here and now, knowing that each situation, each interaction, may never come again. You begin to sharpen your awareness, appreciate more, and engage deeply with your experiences. Being present makes your life feel full.

To really be present, you have to listen to the people you are talking with—not just hear the words spoken, but process them, understand them, and feel them. It means stepping away from your personal agenda and opening yourself up to what the moment offers. It's about absorption; like a sponge soaking in water, you soak in the environment, the conversation, and the emotions around you.

Engaging in this way transforms ordinary interactions. Being present isn't a passive state of being; it's an active, conscious choice to connect, understand, and empathize. And it's in these moments of true connection that you will make deep emotional bonds. These bonds not only affect you personally, but they can change the lives of those around you just as powerfully.

The Antidote to Disconnection

I've learned the hard way that people often don't need solutions or quick fixes; they simply need someone to listen and hear them. Being present is the key to overcoming disconnection. What you can perceive when you're truly in the moment is astonishing. Shifting from a life of constant, mindless activities to one where you're fully present in the moment isn't one giant leap, but a series of small steps that you practice until they become second nature.

It's important to carve out time to genuinely feel and experience. This isn't just about being present; it's about making the path to get there.

Work on intentionally slowing down your pace so you can start to change your internal dialog. When you pause and concentrate on one thing, your entire attention is captured, making it hard to be distracted by other thoughts. These moments make even the smallest details relevant, and time becomes precious.

The goal is to reach a point where simple sights—puppies, ducks, flowers, or even the gentle flow of water—stir an emotional connection. It's not about being overwhelmed with emotion, but about recognizing how lucky you are to be alive and able to enjoy these experiences. It's a celebration of your senses, a gratitude for the eyes that see, the nose that smells, and all the abilities you have that allow you to fully experience the world around you.

PRACTICAL TIPS TO UNLOCK THE SATISFIED LIFE

Intentionally choose to be present.
Make a deliberate choice to be in the moment. Say it out loud if you have to. Ask yourself: How would I be living today if I knew this would be my last week on this earth?

Let the little things matter.
It takes time to notice small details all around you. They add depth and richness to your life, so it's worth taking the time to soak up all those little details around you and appreciate them.

Minimize distractions.

Set aside the time-wasting activities that keep you too busy to think and feel deeply. Resist the urge to multitask. When you multitask, nothing you do gets your full attention and effort, and everything suffers.

Don't let FOMO (fear of missing out) rule your life.

In our information-rich world, it's easy to feel like you're missing out when you're not connected. But quantity is not the same as quality. By constantly dwelling on all the information "out there," you are missing out on the beauty right in front of you, on the special, one-on-one relationships, on the feelings of joy, awe, and gratitude that spring up when you are soaking up the life all around you. Don't let FOMO rob you of that.

Be willing to step out of your comfort zone.

It's okay to risk disrespect or even rejection. By stepping out and connecting with others, starting conversations, and showing your true self, you find strength and resilience. Embrace the discomfort; you may be pleasantly surprised to find that this is where growth and connection happen.

Embrace all emotions.

It's natural to shy away from pain or hurt, but should we avoid hurt at all costs? What if you were able to use that hurt to make yourself stronger? Acknowledge and learn from your negative feelings. They won't last forever, and they can be powerful tools for growth and positivity.

Develop "rituals."

I know a couple who go for a walk together every single morning. They have carried out this routine for 21 years! Imagine the amazing bond they have developed over the years and how rich their mornings must be.

Consider developing daily or weekly activities that add significance to your life, like taking a daily walk in nature, jotting down things you're grateful for, or dedicating regular time to loved ones. Create moments in your day that are full of meaning, beauty, and life.

Decide to live without regrets.

Living with regrets will cause a surprising amount of stress in your life. When you carry around a bunch of "I should haves" or "I wish I hadn'ts," that weight can be pretty heavy, and you'll use up a lot of your energy needlessly.

Focus on the present. Seize opportunities as they arise, appreciate and uplift those around you, and remember that we rarely get chances to redo moments once they've passed.

Connect through storytelling.

Stories have the ability to keep both the speaker and the listener present by focusing all the attention on the story. If the other person is listening to your story, they're naturally going to connect, and now you both are present, setting aside each other's individual agenda. It also helps us relate to each other.

Have real conversations as often as you can.

In a world dominated by technology, genuine discussions are becoming rare. Our conversations often consist of disjointed text or email messages. Make an effort to have meaningful, face-to-face conversations. Looking someone in the eye and truly listening can make them feel valued and heard. Prioritize honest, heartfelt dialogue.

Wrap-Up and Next Steps

In today's whirlwind of a world, it's all too easy to fall into a robotic routine where we're physically there but emotionally distant. It's common to see people zoning out, choosing distractions over genuine experiences. They're missing out on their own lives, let alone the lives of those around them.

Yet, a simple shift in focus can open up a whole new way of seeing life. Imagine this: beauty and kindness everywhere you look, meaningful connections with others, and relationships that fill your heart. Peace and fulfillment aren't just far-fetched dreams; they're within your grasp. All it takes is the decision to slow down and immerse yourself in the here and now, fully engaging with everything that moment has to offer.

By prioritizing human connections, offering a listening ear, and suspending judgment, ordinary encounters can transform into meaningful moments that enrich your life. Slow down and soak up every aspect of the present moment.

Stay engaged through the ups and downs, the rough and the smooth. Treasure each instant because it's unique and irreplaceable. Genuinely absorb, feel, and connect with everything and everyone because that makes you grow.

Being present, loving people unconditionally, and making them feel like a priority are the building blocks to genuine, loving relationships that fill you with strength and gratitude. When you make others feel safe, they're able to be authentic and vulnerable with you in return. By extending a hand, sharing a smile, and being the person who chooses connection over convenience, you get to truly experience life as you live it.

Remember that everything in your life—the joys and the sorrows—molds you into the person you are now. So don't shy away from it. No more evading reality, no more self-made distractions. Choose to be fully present and fill your life with meaningful memories that you won't forget.

CHAPTER 6

TAP INTO THE POWER OF GRATITUDE

"Gratitude can transform common days into
thanksgivings, turn routine jobs into joy, and change
ordinary opportunities into blessings."

—WILLIAM ARTHUR WARD

The ocean was a canvas of beauty, but as I stood there gazing at the waves, I couldn't see past my own cloud of depression and despair.

Just hours ago, I had left Mia, my beautiful 15-year-old daughter, at a wilderness program in Hawaii. The program was designed for youths who had experienced trauma. At first, she didn't want to go (what teenager is excited to leave behind technology?), but she later shared that she was thankful she went.

For weeks leading up to leaving her in the capable hands of the counselors, I'd been carrying the weight of guilt and self-blame. I felt like I hadn't been there for Mia when she needed me most. The painful goodbye I had just gone through was the icing on the cake.

For days, everything seemed to be going so fast, amplifying my sense of helplessness. I had been spinning out of control over the problem—everything seemed so complicated, and my obsessing over the problem made it worse. Now, I couldn't see past this moment. Fifteen years of Mia's life was condensed into this one day. I couldn't see anything else. I couldn't experience anything. I couldn't "just decide to be happy."

I was stuck in a downward spiral of beating myself up. I was a failure, a screw-up. I was angry and utterly defeated. The world felt broken. I began reciting to myself everything that was wrong with the world. I felt trapped.

But now, as I walked on the beach, the breathtaking scene before me began to work its magic. The sun reflecting on the waves sparkled like a million little diamonds. Pacific green sea turtles sunned themselves on the warm sand. Looking out over the water, I spotted a whale just beginning to breach.

As I drew in a deep breath and focused on the beauty around me, everything suddenly slowed down. Mia's life was no longer encapsulated in a single day. Her journey stretched out before me as I began to remember individual frames of the movie of her life.

Memories of holding that fragile newborn, watching her grow, cheering her on as she learned to walk, cherishing her handwritten notes, being enchanted by her delight as she held a little bird in her hand or swam with dolphins. Our adventures, her discoveries, her impact on our world—it all resurfaced.

Nature, in its gentle way, unraveled my knotted emotions and refocused my lens. It brought the beauty back into an ugly situation. As gratitude swelled within me, my perspective shifted.

Our difficulties would turn into strengths. The past was behind us, and I was filled with hope for the future. I stopped judging our history and started appreciating HER STORY. Every experience—even the tough ones—was a gift.

Nature allowed me to slow down and get a new perspective, but gratitude was the tool that reshaped my entire outlook and changed my day.

Getting to Gratitude

Our society isn't very good at feeling and expressing gratitude. It doesn't come naturally to most of us because it's easier to see what we don't have than to take the time to acknowledge what we do have.

We tend to overanalyze our fears and ignore the things that make us happy. Maybe that's a throwback to our survival instincts when we were always on the lookout for threats and problems. People everywhere—especially in the media—seem to reinforce and amplify the negative while downplaying the positive.

For a significant portion of my life, I was surrounded by people who were steeped in this negativity. Their sense of entitlement, unhappiness, rudeness, and complaining drained the life out of me, and I just thought that's how the world was. But when I began to live my truth with intentionality and presence, fully feeling all the emotions that came my way, I started radiating gratitude. This attitude was infectious, and people began reflecting it back to me.

Today, I surround myself with people who are grateful, who enjoy life, and who are happy for every moment. The emotional atmosphere is so different in my inner circle now. It's drama-free and less complicated.

People who are living a Satisfied Life decide not just to survive but to thrive. One signpost of this choice is that their lives are filled with gratitude. At some point, they settle on a mindset of gratitude. They practice thankfulness over and over and, eventually, learn how to find the good in all situations. Being thankful becomes second nature to them.

The real question is: how do we change our mindset? Shifting our emotions from negative to positive isn't as simple as flipping a switch. When we're really hurting, "Don't worry, be happy" feels hollow.

How, then, do we develop a genuine sense of gratitude? That day on the beach after dropping off my daughter, gratitude was the furthest thing from my mind. I was simply taking a deep breath and getting absorbed in the nature around me. I was allowing my thoughts to slow down and align with the bigger picture. In that context, my problem no longer had such a tight grip on me.

When we reflect on our lives and remember the highs, not just the lows, gratitude begins to take root. Negative feelings start to dissipate, making room for thankfulness. What you focus on will grow. Gratitude, once ignited, tends to multiply. A heart full of gratitude can find joy in even the smallest moments.

It becomes increasingly hard to entertain feelings of anger, sadness, or resentment when you're actively seeking out and celebrating the good that happens in your life. When you choose the uncomplicated versus the complicated, your truth versus your untruth, life changes on all levels. Yes, you will encounter challenges, but are you going to focus on one bad chapter in the expansive book of your life?

I made my choice. What will you choose?

Level Up Your Game by Asking Yourself "WHY"

When you live a Satisfied Life, gratitude has to run deeper than mere words. It's not just about saying the right things; it's about genuinely feeling them. This sense of appreciation sinks right to the core of your being. This is why pausing, taking a breath, and reflecting on your life's journey is essential. You need these moments to shut out the world's chaos and to genuinely recognize the blessings and the open doors that have come your way. Such awareness develops a deeply rooted sense of gratitude.

I like to play a game with people: When they tell me they are thankful for something, I ask, *"Why* do you feel that way?" It's a question that demands introspection. Our lives nowadays move at such a rapid pace that we seldom take the time to process our gratitude. But if you can take time to genuinely feel and understand why you're thankful, I guarantee your life will shift to an entirely new level of satisfaction.

The Real Comparison Game

One of the biggest barriers to gratitude is comparison. Society tries to get us to constantly measure ourselves against others, drawing attention to what we lack. This perspective can make us feel cheated, inadequate, and unsuccessful. Such feelings breed insecurity and a sense of defeat.

But when we feel down about ourselves, we tend to make choices that aren't in our best interest.

Some might resort to neglecting their health by sacrificing sleep, indulging in excessive alcohol, or engaging in other harmful habits because it's a temporary escape from the negative feelings. Others might compensate by flaunting their achievements or belittling those around them. All of these faulty coping mechanisms can lead to living beneath our potential, deteriorated health, and damaged relationships with the very people who love us most.

How do we break free from that destructive cycle? Most of us have unconsciously made comparisons throughout our lives. If we're bound to compare, why not turn it to our advantage?

Instead of trying to eliminate comparisons completely, try refocusing through the lens of gratitude. It's easier to transition from a deficit-focused mindset to one that values the assets in our lives. Even if you believe you don't have much, countless others out there dream of having what you possess.

If you're reading this book, you have the ability and desire to grow, learn, and be even better. You have opportunities to step into, and you have relationships to develop. You have a body that, while perhaps not in perfect shape, offers you some level of well-being. Life may be far from ideal, but don't let that stop you from seeing what you do have.

You can appreciate the simple pleasure of watching a bird playing in a puddle, knowing that somewhere, someone is watching a loved one battle a grave illness. And while you may not be independently wealthy, perhaps you have a job that provides for your family and lets you be present for your children, giving you time to have a healthy home life.

Yes, you have challenges. Nobody gets through this life without experiencing pain, sadness, and difficulty. Take heart—you're not alone.

Pause right here and take a deep breath. Do you know what a miracle that is? Just ask someone with emphysema who is on oxygen full time because they can't get enough air. Your heart will beat about 100,000 times today, pumping life into every cell in your body. At this very moment, your mind is active, pondering, and evolving. All miracles!

It's easy to take it all for granted. If you can acknowledge these gifts, you will be rich in a way that money can't buy.

You Can Find the Good In Every Situation

The day my daughter was born, I was overflowing with gratitude. That's a pretty easy thing to be grateful for, isn't it? But what about our failures and mistakes? What about the times when we've been wronged or the moments that bring sadness?

Even those moments can be redeemed for something beautiful. Even in times of difficulty or high stress, gratitude can overpower our negative emotions. Those negative feelings should be acknowledged, but eventually, those emotions lose strength, and gratitude can take over.

The truth is that our most significant growth comes from our failures, not our successes. This growth, however, only occurs if we're willing to reflect on the experience and extract wisdom from it.

Take, for instance, the custody battle I faced for my daughter. I made some glaring mistakes, which came at a high cost. At the time, I couldn't find a shred of gratitude for these blunders. But as time went on and I got some emotional distance, I began to realize that these experiences taught me who I wanted to become and, more importantly, who I *didn't* want to become. They revealed to me an inner strength and resilience I didn't know I possessed. Today, I'm thankful for those challenges because they shaped me into a better man.

Similarly, even profound grief can inspire gratitude. Have you ever lost someone dear to you, and you were filled with a deep appreciation for the precious time that you shared with them? Did you gain a new perspective on how short life can be—that our time here on earth is limited? Did that perspective give you a fresh determination to live life to the fullest, without compromise? By cherishing those memories and living your life to the fullest, you honor that loved one.

And then there are lessons learned vicariously through the struggles of others. I'm reminded of a man who works out at my health club. I told his story in Chapter 4. Even though he was born with only one arm, he never dwells on his limitations. Instead, he radiates positivity, always wearing a smile. Every time I see him, he brings me back to earth, reminding me to put aside my minor grievances and embrace the sheer joy of being alive and active.

Life, in all its complexities—the good, the bad, and the in-between—shapes our journey. Every event, every twist and turn, is an opportunity for growth. And gratitude? It's the lens through which we can recognize and cherish this growth. It gives us a reason to celebrate the gift of another day.

PRACTICAL TIPS TO UNLOCK THE SATISFIED LIFE

Be present.

The flood of information our electronic devices bring can lead to distraction and detachment. Don't let your time slip away in the sea of screens, social media, and games. Put down the phone or whatever mind-numbing distraction has a hold on you, embrace your thoughts, and begin to appreciate life's subtle wonders. Don't miss the beautiful details!

Slow down.

Our modern world grants us the ability to achieve more than ever before, but at the cost of living a hectic and chaotic life, often lost in someone else's narrative. Immerse yourself in nature and allow yourself to slow down. Spend some time with your own thoughts. By doing so, you gain perspective and clarity about your life.

Reflect and cherish.

You are a gift to this world. Be grateful for that gift. Revisit your life's journey regularly. During the week, try jotting down things you're thankful for each day. At the end of the week, review the list. You'll likely find that life is richer than you realized. And now, you have a list of memories you can quickly recall to fill you with gratitude and comfort during difficult times.

Stay open to possibilities.

The world is filled with voices dictating how we should think, feel, and act. It's easy to get bogged down by negativity. Rather than getting flooded with anxiety, focus on what brings joy and gratitude into your life. Stay open to the things that make you happy and fulfilled.

Practice gratitude daily.

You can practice gratitude at any time of the day. If you're not already in the habit of practicing gratitude, you could set an alert on your phone as a reminder throughout the day to connect to this powerful emotion. Eventually, your thought life will transform, and gratitude will become second nature.

Be with people who live a life of gratitude.

You've probably heard it said that you are who you hang out with. There's a lot of truth to that—emotions have a ripple effect. Being around negative or complaining people can pull you into their emotional state. If you aspire to feel gratitude and happiness, surround yourself with those who actively choose these emotions.

Choose gratitude, even in adversity.

If you're in a high state of stress due to external circumstances, finding what there is to be grateful for in those moments makes all the difference. It could be what decides your next move. If you focus on what you perceive to be bad, the stress can catapult you into anxiety and overwhelm. Or, you can access peace and perseverance by identifying what you're grateful for and expressing your gratitude out into the world.

This includes gratitude for what you've accomplished up until now, who you intrinsically are, and what you're meant to do on this earth. Don't resent the cards you've been dealt. Recognize the value in them and be grateful for the opportunity to transform. God made you exactly the way you are for a reason, and the sooner you see and acknowledge that, the better off you'll be.

Choose gratitude, even when others don't.

Life presents challenges, and we inevitably encounter difficult people. When faced with such individuals, protect your peace. Don't let their negativity hover in your mind and emotions like a black cloud. Simply decide to sidestep the drama and lean on cherished memories instead. Look for the good—it's there somewhere.

Express your gratitude.

Simple acts of courtesy—like saying thank you or showing appreciation for gestures—amplify gratitude. A grateful disposition is transformative. When you act entitled, you block potential blessings. But gratitude? It makes life richer. It's an emotion that allows us to truly immerse ourselves in the moment. So, when you feel that impulse to express thanks but hesitate, go ahead and voice it. Gratitude, like respect, often brings more opportunities. And remember, much like a smile, gratitude costs nothing but rewards you with plenty.

Wrap-Up and Next Steps

When I think back to the story at the beginning of this chapter, I remember that moment standing on the beach. I had a choice to make: continue down the dark path of guilt, anger, and despair, or stop feeding those negative emotions and let my thoughts change course. There was so much beauty on the beach that day, but the most beautiful thing was the change that was going on in my heart. Nature allowed me to slow my thoughts down and let them go. I was able to breathe again, to hope, and the resulting gratitude completely overwhelmed me.

It might be natural to zero in on life's imperfections, but it's within your power to stop fueling the negativity and instead shift to finding the good in every situation. The world is full of positivity and beauty, but spotting them requires an intentional effort. It's tempting, especially during trying times, to get bogged down by setbacks and forget about all of the beauty surrounding you. You have to make a conscious decision to slow down and redirect your focus toward appreciation.

You have the power to mute the incessant noise, the distractions, and society's endless control. To embrace nature, be present, slow down, and give yourself the freedom to define your own truth. To cherish the life you've been given and make it a habit to let others know how much you appreciate them. To surround yourself with like-minded people who want to make the most of their lives.

To choose a life of gratitude. This is *your* time, right now!

CHAPTER 7

FIND YOUR "WHY"

"When something is important enough, you do it even
if the odds are not in your favor."

—ELON MUSK

On a recent vacation with my family, I found myself sharing a beautiful moment with my dad. We were sitting on the deck of a yacht. The sky was a gorgeous shade of blue, and there was just enough breeze to keep us cool while we soaked up the warm rays of sunshine. The boat gently rocked in the waves, filling us with a sense of calm and peace.

My dad started reflecting on his life, sharing stories of struggle and triumph. He talked about how my grandfather didn't want to die in a war; he wanted to live and raise a family. That was his "why," so he left everything he knew behind in Macedonia and came to the United States with practically nothing.

He started with so little, but his "why" to build a life and take care of his family guided his every decision. It was his North Star. Two generations later, here we were, building on the foundation of his "why." He was the architect of a powerful legacy that is woven into our own lives today. What a gift!

Let me ask you this: What will your story be? What will your children and grandchildren be saying about you? What will your relationship with them be like? What will you have taught them? How can you live in a way that will make them proud to be walking in your footsteps?

Remember, the journey is just as important as the destination. It might be even more important. Your destination can change over time, but your "why" will always guide you, helping you sculpt each day with purpose and meaning.

Let Your "Why" Light Your Way

Life is not merely about existing but about moving, growing, and being intentional in your actions. As you walk this journey of life, you'll come across countless crossroads. The most reliable guide you'll ever have is understanding your "why."

Your "why" isn't just a fleeting thought or a simple curiosity. It's the fire in your belly, the motive behind every decision, every action, every leap of faith you take. And while every choice you make doesn't need a dramatic backstory, knowing why you are doing something creates clarity for your decisions. It's a clear guide when everything seems uncertain.

Think of people you know who seem lost, dissatisfied, or unfulfilled. Many times, their struggle is less about their circumstances and more about not anchoring themselves to their "why." Lacking this foundation often leaves them paralyzed by fear and doubt, or worse, making choices that end up causing pain for themselves or the people they care about.

Life is a rollercoaster. All of us, no exceptions, will face moments of pain, confusion, and absolute chaos. It's during these moments that it becomes too easy to lose our way. But having a clear "why" acts like a tether, keeping us connected to our goals, our dreams, the very reason that we feel we've been put on this planet.

When you're clear about your "why," you're no longer floating aimlessly—you're moving forward with purpose, and you can always keep your destination in view.

Your "Why" Will Change

As we experience different seasons in our lives, our "whys" can shift and evolve, highlighting various facets of ourselves.

When we're kids, it's simple. We want to be safe. We want to be happy. We run freely, guided by our hearts. Fast forward a few years to young adulthood, when the most important thing becomes fitting in or gaining some independence. With each new milestone along our journey, our priorities and motivations shift.

And with each transition to a new season of life, our "why" can either draw us closer to our true selves or lead us astray as we're caught up in what others think success looks like. But it's not physically or mentally sustainable to live out someone else's vision.

When I was younger, my driving force was simple—to win my dad's approval. I joined the family business, gave it my all, and got plenty of pats on the back. The validation felt amazing, but the work I was doing didn't quite touch my soul. I was borrowing my dad's dream instead of living out my own.

I was going through the motions to appear successful, but I didn't feel fulfilled, confident, or content. So, I plugged the holes in my soul with external rewards and validation. I made risky choices and threw money around to impress my "friends," who I had chosen for all the wrong reasons.

Look Inward

Isn't it easy to get swayed by external influences in situations like this? We can't see anything beyond our own situations and needs. We need validation from others because we aren't aware of our own unique value in this world. We sometimes feel incomplete, so we chase after things that society says are important. The hot car, the impressive bank balance, the latest gadget—symbols of success that promise to impress—that's what society tells us will make us happy, right?

Or perhaps you've felt the weight of others' expectations, or maybe someone told you in the past that you couldn't accomplish something, so you're on a quest to prove them wrong. If your drive comes from a place like that, move past it. If your "why" is driven by that external focus and proving the naysayers wrong, it won't be as fulfilling as something that resonates with your core.

For a while, I was so distracted by "success" and pleasing others that I never really looked at myself in the mirror and asked some hard questions. I forgot about what was important to me, what truly made me happy.

But then Mia, my daughter, burst into my world, and the game changed entirely. Exotic cars dimmed in importance. Money was necessary, but it was just a tool and no longer my identity. As I released the stress of living up to everyone else's ideals and expectations, I experienced a feeling of safety and security because I was finally focusing on myself and my own "why." My identity was shifting, and my "why" was changing right along with it.

As Mia's dad, I had a revelation. If I was going to give her the best of me, I had to find out who the best of me really was. I had to start living on my own terms. I had to set aside the Alex that society and my upbringing had created in order to figure out who I was and who I wanted to be. I had to start asking the hard questions: Who was I really? Why was I here? Who do I want to be? What kind of dad do I want to be? What kind of legacy do I want to leave in this world? Will my legacy remain long after my name is forgotten?

Taking care of Mia redefined my "why." It aligned me with my passion, giving me a clear sense of identity and purpose. She helped me transform the meaning of my life back to its pure, child-like essence, free from the clutter and white noise of everyone else's expectations.

I was able to focus on my purpose beyond any pain I had experienced. I learned I could be happy right there, in the moment, fully present and alive. But most importantly, I realized that I could take all that I was learning and give it away to help others.

It took a while, but I eventually learned that if you drink from the cup of power and money, you'll never be satisfied.

Passion, Purpose, and Possibilities

If passion is the vehicle and the fuel to move you forward along the path of your life, then think of your "why" as the anchor for your passion. When you are firmly anchored to your passion and purpose, it leads to possibilities. You can explore those possibilities because your "why" will protect you from drifting away among the distractions and noise around you. It carves out a clear path for your passion to flow into the things that matter to you most.

In a world constantly whispering what you should want, what you should chase, and who you should be, knowing your "why" keeps you grounded. It keeps you from getting blown off course by things that don't really matter in life.

You can be the smartest or richest person on the planet, but without a clear understanding of your "why," there's a risk that one day you'll look in the mirror and not recognize the reflection staring back, feeling emptiness even in a life that seems to have everything.

Being part of something greater, understanding that bigger picture and where we fit in—that's the stuff of magic. When we harness our "why" and let our passion flow toward it, life stops being a series of tasks. It transforms into a purposeful journey, rich with meaning and direction.

A Force for Good

Discovering your "why" is more than just pinpointing a reason or motive—it's a journey to the heart of your true self. Not all motivations and desires come from the same place. Some are fleeting impulses, and it's easy to act out those desires without thinking about long-term consequences. Other "whys" are deeply rooted callings. It's important to know the difference between the two.

Anything I do in life, my number one rule is to make sure I don't hurt myself. A true "why" you can build your life on is not destructive for you or your loved ones.

When ambitions steer you toward paths that inflict pain—be it physical, mental, or spiritual—it's a sign to reconsider. Life is too precious to sabotage yourself or others, and it can take a long time to "undo" an impulsive decision. Every goal has multiple paths, so it might be wise to seek an alternative route, one that aligns better with the person you aspire to be.

Consider your daily routine. How often do you think about the driving forces behind your actions? Are you chasing material success or the fleeting approval of others, or are you finding purpose and meaning in your days? How are you, in your own unique way, making the world just a touch brighter than you found it?

You're not just an isolated being; you're connected to everyone around you. You have immense power in this connection. You can lift up others and make their lives better, but you can also deflate and tear them down. Recognize this strength within you.

A genuine "why" that aligns with your true self will naturally guide you toward being that force for good wherever you go. That force acts as a multiplier, amplifying the good you bring into the world.

Person to Person, Soul to Soul

Can I single-handedly eradicate world hunger? No. Can I quell a global pandemic, forge world peace, or solve any massive global issue? Unfortunately, no. But here's what you and I can do: We can change our own world right in front of us and positively influence anyone we meet.

Think of a time when you were the target of someone's rudeness or hate. It dragged you down and darkened your day. It's hard to enjoy and appreciate life from that place.

Now, flip the script and remember a time when someone treated you well and made you feel good. It might have been a simple gesture, but if you were feeling down, that simple action had a profound impact.

You and I have that power every single day. You can wake up with the expectation of changing someone's life for the better that day.

You can vow to transform lives, one interaction at a time.

I can smile at somebody on the street and instantly turn their day around. I can get them to laugh. I can encourage, listen, and give love to someone who feels surrounded by a sea of haters.

That's how you and I can impact our world—person to person, soul to soul. And that force for good inspires others to step up and do the same right back to us and to other people who cross their paths, creating a chain of positivity.

Life is so much richer when we're pouring out love and life instead of spewing out problems and hate. Embrace this idea, and watch your world transform, one heartfelt connection at a time.

PRACTICAL TIPS TO UNLOCK THE SATISFIED LIFE

Start a genuine dialogue with yourself.
What activities bring you joy and positively affect those around you? What passions are you ready to invest time into? This isn't a moment for judgment, just for heartfelt honesty. Identify your driving desires and envision a life full of meaning.

Remind yourself of your "why" and start living it immediately.
Once you identify your "why," pursue it relentlessly. After all, life is too short for anything less. Society always tells you what you can't do, but what do your deepest desires tell you that you *can* do? Listen to those desires, and then just *do* it.

Stay in your lane and fully embrace it.

You can't be all things to all people. Once you define your "why," stay focused, do what you are called to do, and do it well.

Trust yourself.

Avoid confining yourself with limitations that stop you from going forward and take your dreams away. How many times has it worked out well for you to confine yourself? Don't over-analyze—go ahead and take that chance. You won't know if you don't try.

Embrace setbacks.

Every setback and failure you face will teach you something. You can take a failure and adjust your course, or you can learn from it and move on. Reframe failure as a positive thing. Choose to be fearless, and remember that the biggest growth often comes from failure.

Commit wholeheartedly and unconditionally to your purpose.

Your "why" can be your compass, especially during challenging tasks. Even in moments of doubt, doing tasks with your "why" in mind can reignite your drive and passion.

Ensure your actions reflect the person you want to be.

When embodying your "why," do so without harming yourself or others. If your path starts altering the foundation of who you are or negatively affects others, pause and recalibrate.

Let your "why" guide you to your destination.

Lacking clarity about your "why" can lead to confusion, and drifting into distractions is all too easy. However, once you understand your "why," let it be your North Star. Dream, plan, and see where your passion takes you.

Turn to your "why" during difficult times.

When you're going through a hard time or your task seems endless, it's easy to lose momentum and stray from your path. Take a moment in those times to remember your "why," and use it to push through the difficult time.

Reevaluate and recalibrate often.

Life is a rollercoaster. With every twist and turn, our desires and values might shift. Keep yourself anchored and on track by consistently checking in with your heart and your "why." Pay special attention to any motives that have shifted or evolved to ensure you are still on the right path.

Wrap-Up and Next Steps

To truly live a life brimming with satisfaction, you must immerse yourself in pursuits that resonate with your heart and soul. Yet, too often, we allow fear of failure or judgment to tether us to the familiar, even when it doesn't serve us.

If you want to chase your dreams and realize the purpose for which you're here, it requires a genuine conversation with yourself. Be honest, peel back the layers, and discover your deepest motives. Find your "why" and let it guide your every move.

The voices from the outside world tell us about boundaries and barriers. But instead of accepting the countless reasons why you can't, search deeply for the reasons why you can—and should. Look at the possibilities.

Your individuality is your strength. The way you approach life—the unique twist you give to every task—is what sets you apart. Remember, no one else can offer the world what you can. You possess a unique blend of talents, insights, and perspectives. There's a magic only you can bring forth.

I invite you to set aside limitations. To sit with yourself and ask some of the most important questions: Why are you here on this earth? What is it that gets you up and stirs your soul each morning? How do you want to show up for the people around you? What motivates you? What fulfills you? What do you want your legacy to be?

And once you've found the answers—your "why"—this is your permission slip to boldly and unconditionally start living according to those motives. No more living small. Go big!

CHAPTER 8

ABOVE ALL, DON'T QUIT

"Life should not be a journey to the grave with the
intention of arriving safe y in a pretty and
well-preserved body, but rather to skid in broadside in
a cloud of smoke, thoroughly used up, totally worn out,
and loudly proclaiming 'Wɔw! What a Ride!'"

—HUNTER S. THOMPSON

What in the world would possess someone to swim for 17 hours straight?

It's 1952, and 33-year-old long-distance swimmer Florence Chadwick is attempting to swim across the Catalina Channel. Imagine watching her in those early-morning hours as she slips into the water, knowing she'll be swimming for the next 15-20 hours to cover the roughly 23 miles back to the California shoreline.

She starts swimming. The water is cold, and the currents pull on her, trying to coax her off course. Hours into her swim, the waves begin to make her feel seasick. She starts to get tired, and her muscles begin to cramp. She's feeling hungry, so every once in a while, she swims over to the boat following her. They hand her a little bit of food and water, but only just enough to keep her going. Then she turns away from the boat and swims toward land.

There are sharks nearby, and as her ear breaks the surface of the water, she hears voices shouting in the boat behind her. Then she hears gunshots—the sharp *bang* echoing off the waves around her. They're shooting at the sharks to keep them from getting any closer to her. But she can't think about that right now. She clears her mind.

Stroke … stroke … stroke … breathe. Just keep swimming.

About 15 hours into her swim, a thick fog settles over them, obscuring everything. Now, the boat moves closer so they don't lose sight of her in the fog. GPS doesn't exist yet. Nobody can see the coastline in the distance. Nobody can tell her how much further she has to go.

The current is strong. Sharks are lurking somewhere below. She's sick, tired, hungry, and she wonders, *How much longer? Did I get lost?* For the first time on this day, she begins to doubt herself.

She pushes ahead for one more hour. Still unable to see the shoreline, she finally gives up and asks to be pulled out of the water.

She is less than a mile from land.

Florence Chadwick may have failed, but she didn't quit. This swim was just a momentary setback. She recovered and returned to swim the channel again two months later. Once again, another thick fog settled over her, but this time, she envisioned the coastline in her mind's eye. She completed the swim in under 14 hours and broke the record—once held by a man.

Failure Is Not the Enemy

Florence Chadwick understood that failure is built into success. She wasn't afraid to fail, and she wasn't willing to give up on her dreams. She knew how to take each failure and use it as a stepping stone to success. In fact, her incredible achievements were a result of learning from failure.

Reflecting on my own life, I see this same principle operating in my family. My dad would always tell us that he was probably the stupidest successful businessman on the planet because he didn't know that quitting was an option. His perseverance was his superpower. Each challenge he faced was another puzzle to solve, another experience to learn from. No setback could stop him, and no failure could scare him away.

He inherited this attitude from his father and, in turn, instilled it in me. He taught me two important concepts: 1. Quitting is off the table, and 2. Failure is not the enemy; it's an ally as long as I use it to "fail forward."

Yes, I was actually taught to fail and use that failure to my advantage. It sounds like a paradox, but there's power in failure!

Quitting Versus Failing (Forward)

Quitting and failing almost sound like the same thing, but they are entirely different! When you quit, you feel ashamed and press the stop button on your journey. You abruptly halt all growth and progress. Failing, on the other hand, is an occurrence, not a state of mind. It's just a tool to move yourself forward because of all you have learned.

Imagine gathering a thousand people in a room and asking them to think of a time when they quit and gave up. "What lessons did quitting teach you?" you'd ask. I bet you'd hear a chorus of voices talking about regret. Sure, they may have learned something—mainly that they shouldn't have quit. But there aren't many lessons left to learn after giving up.

Quitting will sabotage your thoughts. It will whisper, "I'm not enough," filling you with self-doubt. Those nagging thoughts will get louder and louder until that's all you hear. Labels will form in your subconscious—quitter, incompetent, weak. It will make you feel like an imposter and will give you excuses to quit the next thing. And the next.

Quitting is a breeding ground for regret, and regret is a cancer that will quietly eat away at your dreams and desires.

But failure is a different story.

Imagine going back to the same thousand people in a room and asking them to recall a time when they failed at something but didn't give up, didn't surrender. "Tell me what you learned from failure?" you'd ask. I can guarantee you there would be more positive responses from this group. Many would say they came out on the other side of the failure stronger, wiser, and more confident in their own abilities. They used their failure to grow through the problem.

Failure is a powerful tool, a stepping stone to move you along your journey. It teaches you to stand on your own two feet. Failure doesn't just build character and resilience; it reveals it. It peels back the layers, uncovering your strength and showing you what you're capable of.

You discover that success isn't built on victories alone—it's built on many different experiences, including failure. And as long as you're "failing forward," it's still a success.

Remember, quitting is a full stop, but failure is just a comma. It's a pause that allows you to catch your breath, recalibrate, and return to your journey armed with lessons, strength, and resilience. Fail, learn, rise, and repeat!

PRACTICAL TIPS TO UNLOCK THE SATISFIED LIFE

Have an attitude of gratitude.

In the middle of a difficult time, take a moment. Breathe in gratitude for the experience, your health, and life itself. This simple act can shift your focus, allowing you to see a realm of possibilities rather than a wall of problems.

Stop asking why, and just do it.

Life's not fair, but what you do with its curveballs defines your journey. Face tough situations head-on. Remember, life is happening *for* you, not *to* you. Embrace its complexities and challenges.

Focus on "can" instead of "can't."

Whether you think you can or you think you can't, you're right. Your words and thoughts help construct your reality. So instead of taking on a victim mentality and saying things like, "Oh, that's too tough," or "I can't do this," start speaking the language of possibility. See failure as simply a new launching point.

Decide to live without regrets.

No matter what hand you've been dealt in the game of life, that hand doesn't dictate the outcome of the game—you do. Play your cards with determination and strategy, not with regret.

Recognize that nothing is permanent.

Everything has its season. Even your emotions will ebb and flow like an ocean tide. Remember that this, too, shall pass. The hits you take in various battles *will* eventually end. Recalibrate, refocus, and keep moving forward with resilience, determination, clarity, and hope.

Stay actively engaged with your life.

Avoid the temptation to disengage from life's battles through procrastination or impulsive distractions. Stay connected, be present, and engage fully until you accomplish your goals.

Take care of yourself.

Failure doesn't feel good. In times of difficulty, prioritize self-care. Get enough sleep, drink lots of water, exercise, get outside and get some sun on your skin, breathe, appreciate the beauty around you, and surround yourself with people who love you and build you up. Staying strong physically and mentally will help you overcome any difficulty.

Recognize that you are "failing forward."

Remember that obstacles are just a part of any journey. Adopt a learner's perspective and ask yourself, "What valuable lesson is hidden here?" Use your insights as stepping stones to a new path or a return to the right one, strengthened with wisdom.

> **Don't be afraid to pivot.**
> Life's an adventure filled with endless paths. If one doesn't work, be ready to pivot. Adaptability is a superpower that keeps your journey exciting and purposeful.

Wrap-Up and Next Steps

Many fictional stories we read follow the framework of the "Hero's Journey." The main character goes on an epic adventure, faces challenges and trials, and is tested in both character and skill. The character learns life-changing lessons from these confrontations and uses these new insights to overcome each problem, emerging victorious and forever changed by the journey.

Sound familiar? This pattern has graced countless pages of novels, movies, and stories. Why? It's not just a structure for fiction—it works so well in stories because it also reflects real life. It's really the story of all of us. Every journey we take follows this same pattern, unless we quit at the first sign of trouble.

The biggest takeaway from the Hero's Journey is that *without obstacles and failure, there is no story.*

You're the chief architect and storyteller of your life, writing each chapter as you go along. Your journey is that of the hero, filled with potential for growth, learning, and transformation. But that evolution only happens if you stay the course.

You grow through what you go through.

Keep running your race. Stumbling blocks are inevitable, but every time you face one, see it as an opportunity. Adjust, learn, grow, and persevere. Flex those mental and physical muscles. Explore the depths of your resilience. Embrace the concept of "failing forward." Remember that every setback is a setup for a comeback.

You can either be a prisoner of your past or a pioneer of your future. Be a pioneer. Move forward and take control of your own journey.

The world is waiting for you to shine. Don't give up! Don't surrender to fear or mediocrity. Instead, keep going and embrace the challenge, ignoring any fear that tries to shut you down. Now is your time to shine your brightest!

AFTERWORD

"It's good to have money and the things that money can buy, but it's good, too, to check up once in a while and make sure that you haven't lost the things that money can't buy."

—GEORGE HORACE LORIMER

Society often celebrates outward success like money, fame, and titles. There's nothing wrong with these goals; they give you something to focus on and can bring a tremendous sense of accomplishment when you achieve them.

I had these goals when I was younger, and I accomplished many of them, but even in the middle of all of the success and money, I wasn't happy. I was expecting to feel fulfilled, but deep down inside, I was lost and empty. All the trappings of my success only served as diversions from a deeper, unfilled void within me.

Thankfully, two mentors stepped into my life, and their wisdom profoundly shifted my perspective. And then, with the most beautiful timing, my daughter came along and gave me the courage to walk away from what I knew and embrace a way of life that has fulfilled me beyond anything I have ever imagined.

Yet, as I travel and speak, I run into people who are living the life I used to have. They are financially successful, driven, outwardly accomplished … and very unhappy. They feel a deep-seated dissatisfaction, and most of them don't even know why. So they chase after happiness, always falling just short of catching it.

I understand this chase. I've lived it, and I've found a better way. I've stopped chasing success and started chasing satisfaction, and I've made it my life's mission to share the secret I've learned: It's all about connecting deeply with yourself, the people around you, and your surroundings. Connecting deeply with yourself and your journey has the power to transform your entire life.

The Recipe for Deep Connections

In order to have deep, profound connections in life, three elements need to be present: safety, trust, and vulnerability.

Safety. Safety starts within ourselves—we own who we are, and we live according to our truth. We know that we can rely on ourselves, no matter the circumstances. It gives us the freedom to explore, appreciate, and fully participate in our lives. This internal safety allows us to be open and authentic with others, who in turn can feel safe to let their guard down, connect with us, and start living their own truth.

Trust. When safety is established, trust can grow. Conversations with others, and even conversations with ourselves, are more meaningful and authentic when they're wrapped in a blanket of trust.

Vulnerability. This is the result of an atmosphere of safety and trust. Being vulnerable allows us to interact at a deeper level because we speak and live honestly, enhancing the quality of our relationships.

Each of these chapters contains tools you can add to your toolbox to connect and develop strong, healthy relationships. We are not created to be solitary. We are meant to be intertwined in each other's lives. We are designed to get out of our heads and turn outward to interact with all the life that is brimming all around us. We are built to give and receive love unconditionally. That's the key to a deeply Satisfied Life.

Carpe Diem—Seize the Day!

In the 1989 movie *Dead Poets Society*, John Keating, an English teacher at an all-boys school, brings his students to a hall filled with pictures and trophies from years past.

As they walk toward a case and look over the black and white photos, Keating says, "... if you listen real close, you can hear them whisper their legacy to you ... Carpe Diem. Seize the day boys, make your lives extraordinary."

There is beauty and significance all around you. You are here for a reason; your existence on this planet holds purpose and value. The world needs your unique gifts, and there are people out there waiting to connect with and be impacted by you. Seize the day!

Live a Story Worth Telling

Take a minute to think about your lineage. You're likely familiar with your parents and grandparents—their quirks, passions, successes and failures, and life stories—because of your direct interactions with them. They are vivid characters in the ongoing story of your life.

But do you know what your great-grandparents were like? How about your great-great-grandparents? Is there a story there, or just a name sprinkled with a few scattered facts and anecdotes?

It's hard to believe that despite our achievements, we might only be remembered in snippets by future generations.

But you possess the power to leave an enduring legacy—not through material achievements or titles, but through the richness of your character and the positive impact you make on others. You have *today*. This very day, you can live your life deeply and touch the people around you. Everywhere you go, you can leave your world better off because you were there, ensuring you live not just in memory but in the stories passed down through generations.

Your life's book is being written with each passing moment. You may have some chapters filled with regret, pages you wish you could rewrite. Those chapters can't be rewritten, but you *can* stop staring at those old chapters and leave them in the past. You can take the lessons you learned from them and shift your focus toward crafting a future filled with intention and authenticity.

Embrace your whole self—the strengths and the flaws. This acceptance liberates you to live truthfully and fully. By clearing your emotional debts, you're positioned to love the journey that unfolds.

So, ponder this: what tales will your descendants share about you? Will they talk about your professional titles and accolades, or will they recount how you made them feel valued, seen, and heard? Will they remember you as an authority figure or as someone who truly touched their lives?

Imagine a chapter where you are celebrated not for your status but for how deeply you influenced those around you. What a profound legacy that would be—a story truly worth telling.

Your Permission Slip

As you read these words, recognize your unique significance. You are important and have the capacity to transform your world. I believe in you.

Consider this your ultimate permission slip to slow down and breathe deeply. To immerse yourself in the beauty that surrounds you and connect meaningfully with family, friends, and even those you encounter briefly.

To let go of society's relentless demands and shifting expectations. To reconnect with what truly nourishes your soul and commit to living your truth without apology.

To honor yourself. To care for your physical, mental, emotional, and spiritual well-being. To embrace your identity wholeheartedly, without excuses, and live with authenticity. To love yourself unconditionally.

This is your permission slip to laugh out loud, allow yourself to feel joy, and experience life as if no one is watching—and if they are, to not care about what they think. To set and follow your own standards so deeply that other people's judgments and expectations no longer have any power over you.

To allow yourself to be vulnerable, secure in the knowledge that your true self is invincible. To be a beacon of strength and resilience. To make others feel seen, heard, and safe in your presence.

To accept your mistakes as inevitable and valuable. To use them to "fail forward" and to focus on being a smarter, wiser, and better person, not in spite of your mistakes, but because of them.

This is your permission slip to pick up your pen and intentionally write your next chapter in the book of your life. To seize each day and live purposefully and marvelously.

To embrace the profound satisfaction of a life well-lived.

ACKNOWLEDGMENTS

Mia: I want you to know that I love you more than anything in the universe, that you are truly an amazing human being, and I'm so happy to call you my daughter. I know you are a person of honor who will stand up for what you believe in. You gave me that permission slip to be unapologetic with my emotions and feelings. You have been my rock and helped me overcome all the attacks that have come at me for speaking my truth. You are an amazing child! Don't ever lose your heart—it's where I get my strength to live fully present and emotional every moment of my life.

Don: Thank you for teaching me the two most important mantras in life and supporting me unconditionally. I will miss you.

Dick: Thanks for being the first person to show me what it felt like to be truly present and for the respect and trust you always gave me.

Renee: Thank you for telling me I was like a Chupacabra—like some mysterious, mythical creature because I didn't behave like most men, and I allowed myself to be emotional, engaging, caring, and unconditional.

Gaby: Thank you for having the understanding of what passion meant to you and letting me know I was an ASSHOLE. I've been a recovering asshole ever since.

Michelle: Thank you for the miracle gift of Mia and the journey that ensued.

My Parents: As I've traveled along this life journey with you, you allowed me to watch how each of you handled the ups and downs of every season in your lives. My front-row seat gave me so much perspective, and you inspired me to be who I am and live my truth with no guilt or remorse. You've helped me to live the fullest life imaginable with no regrets. Thank you.

My Love: Thank you for being such an amazing woman, so alive, present, supportive, tough, wise, and unconditional. Thank you for being filled with love, nurturing, caring, and empathy, but most importantly, for being completely drama-free, which enabled me to be the best version of myself to write this book.

Tim Storey: Thank you for letting me know and showing me firsthand what it felt like to change a person's perspective on life, helping them find their way and come alive with purpose.

John York: You taught me that all that mattered was my truth and to turn off the outside drama. You fought for me, and your legacy is my wonderful relationship with my daughter. Thank you.

Dr. Carol Lindquist: I don't have enough words to express how thankful I am that you were so devoted to your craft and cared unconditionally with such a maternal instinct. You taught me more about the human mind than anybody could ever imagine, and your influence in my life will live on always.

Josh Brown: Thank you for introducing me to my publishing team. You are the catalyst for helping me develop my manifesto through the book-writing process.

Kathy Haskins: I don't have enough words to explain my gratitude. You took my words and made this book come alive, and you showed me the gift that I had. Writing this with you truly made me feel blessed to be your friend. There's no way this book could have been as excellent as it feels and sounds without your help.

Lori Lynn: Your editing made this book come alive, and your devotion, passion, and love for bringing someone's story to life is truly an amazing gift. A picture may paint 1,000 words, but I think this book paints 1,000 pictures.

Shanda Trofe: Thank you for your invaluable guidance. You took my raw manuscript and turned it into a beautiful book that I'm proud to call mine.

A final thank you to everyone who told me thank you for impacting their lives and telling me that I must write this book. Thank you for encouraging me to go out there and spread my message. I am so thankful for each one of you.

ABOUT THE AUTHOR

The founder of Satisfied Life, Alex Peykoff watched his entrepreneurial father and then brother build Niagara Bottling into the largest privately owned beverage company in the world.

Surrounded by the trappings of success from a young age—wealth, influence, and recognition—he had it all by society's standards. Despite all the external success, he felt a profound emptiness inside. He was "rich on paper, poor in life."

He eventually realized that true fulfillment couldn't be measured by financial achievements alone. There was a deeper level of satisfaction that he yearned for—one that aligned with his core values and brought meaning to his life.

Now, he's dedicated to helping others do the same.

Today, Alex serves high-achieving entrepreneurs, successful professionals, and those who are seeking more meaning in their lives. Through his live events, one-on-one coaching, and mastermind group, he helps his audience clarify their vision, overcome obstacles, and leverage their success into a life filled with purpose and satisfaction.

A successful author, speaker, coach, entrepreneur, and real estate developer, Alex describes himself as a "recovering asshole." Thankfully, two mentors entered his life, helping him break his destructive cycles and unlock his emotional toolbox. Then came Mia, his daughter, a 7-pound, 8-ounce force that pushed him to radically transform himself into the best "Dadom" he could be.

Born in Newport Beach, California, and a proud graduate of Chapman University, Alex is the founder of the Satisfied Life Foundation, dedicated to healing trauma and cultivating resilience in teens who've endured abuse and hardship.

Find out more at **AlexPeykoff.com**.

ACCESS YOUR FREE GIFT HERE

Are You Ready to Be Emotionally Debt-Free?

To find out if your emotional health aligns with your values, take the short *Satisfied Life*

Emotional Well-Being Assessment.

As a bonus, schedule your free
15-minute consultation with Alex.

Simply scan the QR code below or visit:

EmotionallyDebtFree.com

www.ingramcontent.com/pod-product-compliance
Lightning Source LLC
Chambersburg PA
CBHW060543130626
46553CB00002B/876